The 2-8-0 Tank Papers

4200 and 5200 2-8-0Ts
4200-4299, 5200-5294

IAN SIXSMITH
Tables by Richard Derry

5225 done up as probably no other 2-8-0T ever was, in lined green as exhibit 41 at Darlington in July 1925.

Irwell Press Ltd.

Acknowledgements

Salvation from traps and snares, running hares halted,
and a guiding hand out of many blind alleys; thanks
to (especially) Eric Youldon, Brian Penney, Brian
Williams, Rob Kinsey, Tony Wright, Peter Coster, Nick
Deacon and Allan Baker.

First published in the United Kingdom in 2017,
by Irwell Press Limited, 59A, High Street, Clophill,
Bedfordshire MK45 4BE
Tel: 01525 861888
www.irwellpress.com

4243 Newport 25/2/16; Aberdare 24/11/17; Newport 22/12/17; Aberdare 25/3/23; Llanelly 7/9/24; Newport Ebbw Jct 19/2/28; Pontypool Road 10/6/28; Aberdare 11/4/31; Newport Ebbw Jct 6/6/31; Aberbeeg 1933; Newport Ebbw Jct 7/4/34; Cathays 23/7/38; Newport Pill 20/8/38; Newport Ebbw Jct 11/11/39; Newport Pill 10/42; Pontypool Road 11/42; Aberbeeg 2/44; Cardiff Canton 8/45; Aberbeeg 19/4/47; Severn Tunnel Jct 23/4/49; Neath 16/5/53; Tondu 21/2/59; Neath 5/9/63; Tondu 28/11/63; Pontypool Road 4/5/64; **w/d 14/5/64; mileage 792,850 as at 28/12/63; sold to J Cashmore, Newport 2/7/64**

4244 Newport 25/2/16; Pontypool Road 30/1/21; Newport Dock Street 30/11/24; Swansea East Dock 25/11/28; Newport Ebbw Jct 23/12/28; Pontypool Road 17/2/29; Newport Ebbw Jct 10/3/34; Newport Pill 19/1/35; **Rebuilt as 7247 9/38**

4245 Newport 6/3/16; Barry 4/10/25; Newport Ebbw Jct 19/1/35; **Rebuilt as 7253 12/39**

4246 Newport 6/3/16; Llanelly 24/11/17; Bristol 22/12/17; Llanelly 6/7/18; Newport 3/8/18; Neath 9/9/23; Duffryn Yard 24/1/26; Neath 8/7/29; Neath 15/2/30; Duffryn Yard 21/11/31; Aberbeeg 10/42; Newport Pill 7/44; Newport Ebbw Jct 28/11/53; Aberbeeg 22/4/61; **w/d 13/11/62; mileage 717,134; sold to Birds, Risca 1/11/63**

4247 Newport 20/3/16; Neath 16/3/18; Newport 13/4/18; Gloucester 14/8/21; Newport Dock Street 11/9/21; Newport Pill 14/4/29; Newport Ebbw Jct 1933; Aberbeeg 28/7/34; Newport Ebbw Jct 25/8/34; Aberbeeg 19/3/35; Cathays 15/10/38; Newport Ebbw Jct 12/11/38; St Blazey 1/11/52; Newport Ebbw Jct 25/1/58; Aberbeeg 22/4/61; Tondu 14/7/62; **w/d 24/4/64; mileage 759,392 as at 28/12/63; sold to Woodham Brothers, Barry; engine preserved**

4248 Newport 24/3/16; Severn Tunnel Jct 22/12/17; Newport 1920; Severn Tunnel jct 12/8/23; Newport 9/9/23; Neath 7/9/24; Swansea East Dock 19/4/25; St Blazey 2/9/28; Newport Ebbw Jct 19/2/35; Llanelly 15/7/61; St Philips Marsh 7/10/61; Severn Tunnel Jct 24/2/62; **w/d 24/5/63; mileage 767,850; sold to Woodham Brothers, Barry 9/10/63; engine preserved at Steam Museum, Swindon**

4249 Newport 12/4/16; Pontypool Road 5/10/24; Newport Pill 10/2/34; Newport Ebbw Jct 17/11/34; Cathays 19/9/36; Newport Ebbw Jct 1/5/37; Tondu 5/3/38; **Rebuilt as 7248 10/38**

4250 Newport 14/4/16; Barry 28/1/23; Trehafod 12/7/25; Landore 29/11/25; Swansea East Dock 2/10/27; Landore 17/10/36; Duffryn Yard 1/11/52; Cardiff Canton 21/2/53; Aberbeeg 17/7/54; Duffryn Yard 31/12/60; Llanelly 12/8/61; **w/d 5/9/62; mileage 860,681; sold to R S Hayes, Bridgend 26/8/63**

4251 Newport 1/5/16; Llanelly 29/9/17; Newport 23/10/17; Aberdare 23/3/24; Newport Dock Street 20/4/24; Aberdare 7/9/24; Aberbeeg 28/12/24; Newport Dock Street 6/9/25; Cathays 2/10/27; Barry 1933; Danygraig 22/9/34; Neath 19/10/35; Aberbeeg 19/9/36; Newport Ebbw Jct 17/10/36; Tondu 15/10/38; Newport Ebbw Jct 9/44; Aberbeeg 6/45; Tondu 22/3/47; **w/d 20/6/63; mileage 766,911; sold to R S Hayes, Bridgend 1/1/64**

4252 Swansea East Dock 24/2/17; Newport 1920; Neath 19/6/21; Swansea East Dock 21/5/22; Neath 15/6/22; Newport 15/6/24; Severn Tunnel Jct 23/1/27; Newport Ebbw Jct 20/2/27; Aberbeeg 1/9/29; Newport Ebbw Jct 29/9/29;; Aberbeeg 27/10/29; Newport Ebbw Jct 22/12/29; Cardiff Canton 26/6/38; Neath 10/42; Llantrisant 21/3/59; Newport Ebbw Jct 7/10/61; Aberdare 6/10/62; Neath 26/1/63; **w/d 30/9/63; mileage 855,380; sold to R S Hayes, Bridgend 1/1/64**

4253 Newport from 5/2/17; Carmarthen 14/4/17; Newport Ebbw Jct 1920; Llanelly 16/11/35; Newport Ebbw Jct 11/1/36; Aberbeeg 19/9/36; Newport Ebbw Jct 17/10/36; Aberbeeg 1/5/37; Newport Ebbw Jct 24/7/37; Newport Pill 14/10/39; w/d 11/4/63; mileage 731,918; **sold to Woodham Brothers, Barry 18/6/63; engine preserved**

4254 Gloucester 17/3/17; Newport 14/4/17; Duffryn Yard 2/12/23; Llanelly 15/6/24; Neath 15/4/28; Danygraig 19/10/35; Llanelly 3/2/40; Pantyffynon 30/3/40; Llanelly 4/40; Pantyffynon 8/41; Llanelly 11/41; Swindon 31/8/52; Cardiff Canton 29/1/55; Newport Pill 24/2/62; Severn Tunnel Jct 29/6/63; Newport Ebbw Jct 26/12/64; **w/d 30/4/64; mileage 865,967 as at 28/12/63; sold to R S Hayes, Bridgend 1/1/64**

4255 Neath 28/3/17; Swansea East Dock 12/5/17; Neath 16/6/22; Swansea East Dock 28/12/24; Danygraig 20/2/27; Swansea East Dock 2/10/27; Duffryn Yard 27/11/27; Swansea East Dock 23/12/28; Danygraig 22/8/36; Cathays 21/8/37; Danygraig 18/9/37; Carmarthen 29/4/39; Danygraig 27/5/39; Duffryn Yard 10/44; Cardiff Canton 10/7/48; Newport Ebbw Jct 27/2/54; Aberdare 16/6/56; Neath 5/9/59; Newport Ebbw Jct 13/4/64; **w/d 20/4/64; mileage 829,470 as at 28/12/63; sold to Birds, Risca 3/6/64**

4256 Newport 5/4/17; Llanelly 7/9/24; Swansea East Dock 19/4/25; Llanelly 9/8/25; Neath 12/5/29; Llanelly 9/6/29; Pantyffynon 1/8/31; Llanelly 29/8/31; Danygraig 1933; Landore 13/1/34; Duffryn Yard 26/2/49; **w/d 22/1/64; mileage 821,282 as at 28/12/63; sold to G Cohen, Morriston 24/3/64**

4257 Newport Ebbw Jct 8/4/17; Newport Dock Street 25/1/25; Newport Ebbw Jct 26/12/26; Aberbeeg 20/3/27; Cathays 2/10/27; Aberdare 20/12/30; Newport Ebbw Jct 4/7/31; Llantrisant 1933; Newport Ebbw Jct 5/3/38; Aberbeeg 3/41; Newport Ebbw Jct 4/41; Newport Pill 2/43; Aberdare 8/45; Neath [o/l] 25/2/61; Newport Ebbw Jct 25/3/61; Aberdare 15/7/61; Llanelly 8/9/62; Aberdare 6/10/62; **w/d 22/10/63; mileage 778,294; sold to R S Hayes, Bridgend 1/1/64**

4258 Newport 21/4/17; Tondu 6/11/21; Barry 23/4/22; Swansea East Dock 27/1/24; Newport Ebbw Jct 19/4/25; Aberdare 17/5/25; Danygraig 15/5/27; Swansea East Dock 12/6/27; Newport Ebbw Jct 7/7/29; Cardiff Canton 7/5/32; Tondu 11/12/37; Aberbeeg 2/4/38; Tondu 5/40; Aberbeeg 2/42; Newport Pill 8/41; Aberbeeg 2/11/57; Newport Pill 25/1/58; Newport Ebbw Jct 3/12/60; Newport Pill 20/4/63; Newport Ebbw Jct 11/7/63; Neath 28/11/63; Aberdare 5/10/64; Severn Tunnel Jct 6/3/65; **w/d 21/4/65; mileage 776,480 as at 28/12/63; sold to Birds, Risca 2/6/65**

4259 Llanelly 7/5/17; Swansea East Dock 19/6/21; Danygraig 9/9/23; Swansea East Dock 28/12/24; Neath 1/11/25; Swansea East Dock 29/11/25; Neath 14/3/31; Swansea East Dock 27/12/52; Newport Ebbw Jct 11/9/54; Aberbeeg 25/2/56; Newport Pill 18/5/57; Newport Ebbw Jct 11/7/63; **w/d 10/3/64; mileage 818,773 as at 28/12/63; sold to Birds, Risca 23/4/64**

4260 Newport 9/5/17; Tondu 9/10/21; Swansea East Dock 28/12/24; Severn Tunnel Jct 26/12/26; Newport Ebbw Jct 23/1/27; Pontypool Road 14/3/31; Newport Ebbw Jct 7/4/34; Severn Tunnel Jct 8/41; Newport Ebbw Jct 5/45; Aberbeeg 8/45; Newport Ebbw Jct 20/4/46; Tondu 25/3/50; Llanelly 29/11/53; **w/d 15/6/59; mileage 786,645; sold to J Cashmore, Newport 5/2/60**

4261 Llanelly 17/7/18; Newport 27/3/21; Llanelly 19/6/21; Barry 22/3/25; Aberdare 1933; Barry 2/6/34; Swansea East Dock 22/9/34; Cathays 9/2/35; Pontypool Road 9/3/35; St Blazey 27/7/35; Laira 21/9/35; Newport Ebbw Jct 11/12/37; Llantrisant 1/42; **w/d 9/3/59; mileage 752,532; sold to Wards, Briton Ferry**

4262 Newport 10/10/19; Danygraig 3/12/22; Swansea East Dock 2/12/23; Danygraig 7/9/24; Swansea East Dock 25/1/25; Newport Ebbw Jct 1/11/25; Aberbeeg 15/2/30; Tondu 9/5/31; Llantrisant 11/8/31; Tondu 26/9/31; Newport Ebbw Jct 4/5/35; Severn Tunnel Jct 8/41; St Philips Marsh 31/8/50; Aberdare 5/10/57; Tondu 1/8/62; **w/d 20/4/64; mileage 756,782 as at 28/12/63; sold to Birds, Morriston 3/6/64**

4263 Newport Ebbw Jct 14/10/19; Tondu 29/11/25; Cardiff Canton 1/9/29; Llantrisant 24/11/29; Cardiff Canton 22/12/29; Llantrisant 15/2/30; Cardiff Canton 15/3/30; Llantrisant 12/4/30; Cardiff Canton 7/6/30; Newport Pill 24/10/31; Newport Ebbw Jct 7/3/36; Newport Pill 19/9/36; Newport Ebbw Jct 4/3/39; Newport Pill 1/4/39; Gloucester 12/41; Newport Ebbw Jct 3/43; Aberbeeg 9/43; Newport Ebbw Jct 2/44; Aberdare 26/3/55; Tondu 8/10/55; **w/d 14/2/64; mileage as at 28/12/63; sold to R S Hayes, Bridgend 24/4/64**

4264 Newport 21/10/19; Swansea East Dock 22/4/23; Llantrisant 21/2/26; Cardiff Canton 21/3/26; Llantrisant 26/9/31; Tondu 21/11/31; Pontypool Road 19/11/32; Aberbeeg 7/41; Pontypool Road 8/41; Aberdare 14/6/47; Neath 8/10/55; Newport Pill 13/8/60; Swansea East Dock 13/6/63; **w/d 29/7/63; mileage 770,281; sold to G Cohen, Morriston 1/1/64**

4265 Newport 30/10/19; Aberbeeg 13/8/22; Newport 10/9/22; Landore 9/9/23; Llanelly 23/1/27; Neath 25/11/28; Landore 9/8/47; Duffryn Yard 31/8/50; Neath 8/10/55; Newport Ebbw Jct 21/5/60; **w/d 24/6/63; mileage 774,189; cut up 2/11/63**

4266 Newport Ebbw Jct 6/11/19; Llantrisant 21/11/31; Newport Ebbw Jct 17/10/36; Aberbeeg 5/2/38; Newport Ebbw Jct 5/3/38; Severn Tunnel Jct 14/10/39; Newport Ebbw Jct 10/41; Neath 9/42; Carmarthen 8/44; Cardiff Canton 12/6/48; Aberdare 13/5/52; Cardiff Canton 18/6/53; Newport Ebbw Jct 21/5/60; **w/d 29/8/62 mileage 781,287; cut up 23/3/63**

4267 Newport 18/11/19; Barry 5/11/22; Trehafod 19/4/25; Barry 17/5/25; Danygraig 6/4/35; Swansea East Dock 1/6/35; Llanelly 21/9/35; Swansea East Dock 19/10/35; Newport Ebbw Jct 12/40; Aberbeeg 4/43; Newport Ebbw Jct 6/43; Aberbeeg 7/43; Pontypool Road 2/44; Aberbeeg 17/5/47; Cardiff Canton 31/7/51; Barry 17/6/52; Newport Ebbw Jct 28/1/56; Llantrisant 31/10/59; **w/d 23/10/62; mileage 710,296; sold to J Cashmore, Newport 18/6/63**

4268 Newport Dock Street 22/11/19; Newport Ebbw Jct 29/11/25; Newport Pill 14/4/29; Newport Ebbw Jct 7/3/36; Newport Pill 25/7/36; Cathays 20/8/38; Aberbeeg 17/9/38; Cathays 20/8/38; Aberbeeg 17/9/38; Newport Ebbw Jct 12/40; Cardiff Canton 4/11/50; Llantrisant 28/11/53; Cardiff Radyr 26/10/64; Aberdare 7/11/64; Newport Ebbw Jct 6/2/65; **w/d 25/8/65; mileage 722,859 as at 28/12/63; sold to J Cashmore, Newport 24/9/65**

4269 Newport Ebbw Jct 30/11/19; Aberbeeg 15/2/30; Newport Ebbw Jct 21/11/31; Newport Pill 14/10/39; Aberbeeg 27/3/54; Tondu 23/3/57; **w/d 19/11/62; mileage 712,683; sold to R S Hayes, Bridgend 26/8/63**

4270 Newport Ebbw Jct 6/12/19; Tondu 16/10/37; Aberbeeg 5/2/38; Tondu 5/3/38; Aberbeeg 10/42; Slough 9/45; Newport Ebbw Jct 26/1/46; Aberbeeg 24/1/48; Cardiff Canton 31/8/50; Cardiff East Dock 8/9/62; **w/d 27/9/62; mileage 773,687; sold to Woodham Brothers, Barry 18/6/63; engine preserved**

4271 Newport Dock Street 19/2/20; Newport Ebbw Jct 26/12/26; Aberbeeg 17/3/29; Newport Ebbw Jct 14/2/31; Aberbeeg 14/3/31; Newport Ebbw Jct 1933; Aberbeeg 13/1/34; Newport Ebbw Jct 22/9/34; Cathays 9/3/35; Newport Ebbw Jct 6/4/35; Pontypool Road 25/12/48; Aberbeeg 30/11/50; Newport Ebbw Jct 21/3/53; Swansea East Dock 13/6/59; Severn Tunnel Jct 16/6/62; Newport Pill 1/12/62; Newport Ebbw Jct 8/8/63; **w/d 16/12/63; mileage 728,528; sold to J Cashmore, Newport 28/2/64**

4272 Newport Dock Street 28/2/20; Swansea East Dock 29/11/25; Duffryn Yard 29/8/31; Swansea East Dock 1933; Neath 3/43; Aberdare 17/5/52; Llanelly 3/10/59; Aberdare 19/5/62; Llanelly 8/9/62; Cardiff East Dock 6/10/62;
w/d 15/10/63; mileage 797,765; sold to R S Hayes, Bridgend 1/1/64

Green 4298 at Saltash in 1948, BRITISH RAILWAYS in serif. This 2-8-0T was one which spent most of its GWR life in the West, only coming 'home' to South Wales in the early 1950s. Derek Clayton.

Below. 4230 newly outshopped at Swindon in 1955. ATC fitted (shoe below buffer beam and conduit along running plate) and note how the vacuum pipe descends vertically from the buffer beam almost to rail level. Some repetition is unavoidable in a series such as these *Papers,* so here goes: *On the right-hand side of some GWR classes (the majority of the GWR 4-cylinder and 2-outside cylinder tender locomotives in fact) there was a long, prominent pipe behind the hand rail, immediately in front of the right-hand cab window. This was the 4-cone ejector. At the back of this substantial pipe was a clack-box, connecting the ejector to the vacuum train pipe. There were also connections to the ejector from the drivers brake valve (DBV) supplying steam to the four cones which created the vacuum. The mixture of steam and air from the train pipe was ejected along the pipe to the smokebox and finally ejected through an annular ring around the base of the chimney into the atmosphere. The drivers brake valve associated with the 4-cone ejector was fitted on to a blank pad on the boiler back plate. In addition to the butterfly valve, which the driver operated to admit air into the train pipe to apply the brake, the DBV incorporated a large, quick action steam valve, which supplied steam from the boiler to the four cones in the ejector to give quick acting evacuation of the train pipe. There was also a small, quick action, steam valve which supplied steam to one of the four cones in the ejector. This was used to maintain the train pipe vacuum when the vacuum pump was not in operation; for example, during station stops. The Manors, 2-6-0s and the tanks however were different, having single cone ejectors. With this arrangement the steam cone was incorporated in the drivers brake valve and the exhaust pipe to the smokebox passed through the boiler to the annular ring under the chimney. This was internal, so there was no prominent pipe along the boiler behind the hand rail; it was made of copper, in contrast to the steel fire tubes. All the vacuum braked tank locomotives were fitted with the single cone ejector; hence no ejector pipe visible on the right-hand side, or visible anywhere for that matter. The DBV in this case had the standard butterfly valve but had only the single large quick action steam valve which supplied steam to the single cone. At sheds, renewal of the steel fire tubes was carried out by the boilersmiths but by some long-forgotten ruling of ancient demarcation, renewal of the copper ejector internal pipe was the responsibility of the fitting staff. This was quite an interesting job because after collapsing and removing the old pipe the new pipe had to be manoeuvred through the tube plate hole and threaded over the boiler tubes towards the corresponding hole in the back plate. Steel fire tubes were rigid but the copper internal pipe was more supple and sagged considerably so it was usually necessary to 'fish'*

for the end of the pipe with a broom handle, or other such sophisticated device, and guide it through the back plate hole. The pipe was expanded into the back plate and tube plate, to make a steam tight joint and the expanding rollers had to be borrowed from the boilersmiths to do this. The pipe on the ground the fitter is looking at under the cab step is the water overflow pipe removed from the right-hand injector, the latter being located under the cab, between the frames. The pipe appearing from behind the tank top, up to the clack box on the safety valve body is the delivery pipe from the injector. There was a similar arrangement on the 7200 2-8-2Ts where the delivery pipe was divided into two sections with a flanged joint up behind the tank. **Rail Photoprint**

4235 at Newport Pill in 1949 with a small-size Gill sans BRITISH RAILWAYS. D.K. Jones Collection.

5263 with block GWR, at Swansea East Dock, 7 July 1947. This is one of the 'new' 5200s, built to replace those rebuilt to 2-8-2Ts and was thus the 'second' 5263, the original having become 7228. Loco still has horizontal (almost) rainstrip. H.C. Casserley, courtesy R.M. Casserley.

Plain and unadorned, 5255 at Swindon in the 1930s. This is the 'original' 5255 and is about to enter the works for rebuilding to 2-8-2T 7220. D.K. Jones Collection.

5236 outshopped in glorious black (not that this will last long) in November 1956 and looking much neater now with curved dropped front ends. Outside steam pipes had appeared from new. E. Trotter, transporttreasury

4235 looking splendid in black at Swindon, 18 November 1956. M.J. Reade, ColourRail

Tondu's 4236, newly arrived from works overhaul and painting, is stabled in the shed yard in 1955. Outside steam pipes (February 1944) but square drop end retained. That safety valve bonnet even looks like polished brass; indeed Caerphilly was known to have turned out a few thus distinguished. A minor marvel, 'polished' not being a word ever associated with the eight-coupled tanks... D.K. Jones Collection.

A couple of Aberbeeg's 2-8-0Ts, 4237 to the fore, with a brake van sandwiched in between, on 16 May 1957. With Target Numbers up, they are either returning from jobs or setting out for one of the collieries in the area. Up above is the A467; the shed was on the west side of the line over on the right. Aberbeeg station is behind the photographer, to the north. The outside steam pipes date from September 1950. Norman Preedy.

A 2-8-0T in its natural setting, weedy sidings draped in coal dust, to a background of moorland and terracing. 4241, on a colliery job at Blaenogwr near Nantymoel at the end of the Ogmore branch on 13 July 1959, was working from nearby Tondu MPD at the time. H.C. Casserley, courtesy R.M. Casserley.

4261 at home at Llantrisant shed, 5 May 1951, in company with pannier 3612 and another 2-8-0T, 5241. 4261 had been at Llantrisant since the War, remaining there through to withdrawal. Newly painted, it has clearly had a Heavy General recently, though as was common in that uncertain period, no lettering has been applied and, in fact, it retains the GW painted number on the buffer beam. In time it got the first emblem, though never the second. H.C. Casserley, courtesy R.M. Casserley.

4262 in an interesting view, poking out of the one oddly extended stall of the Tondu roundhouse on 21 July 1963. It is not clear what purpose this served but it was original, dating from the shed's origins under Dean in the 1880s and surviving the rebuilding of the shed which saw the fitting of this new modern roof in the 1940s. Perhaps it was useful to move engines out of the way that were under repair. L. Turner, transporttreasury

4264 with an eastbound freight on the down through at Cardiff General in April 1958; outside steam pipes and curved drop running plate, fitted April 1944. Behind at platform 2 is 6834 DUMMER GRANGE. Norman Preedy.

4265 in quite respectable condition for a 2-8-0T, with second emblem, at Gloucester Horton Road MPD on 11 April 1962. The chalking by the doorway says ALL OUT presumably referring to the fire some time previously. The water levelling pipe behind the cab steps, connecting the side tanks with the third tank under the coal space, was described under 4267 in the introductory notes and clearly here, on 4265, the pipe has disappeared. They were prone to fracturing and had to be taken down for the fracture to be welded, the loco unable to return to service until it had been refitted and the tanks refilled. A BR 1952 drawing, 132221, is labelled 'experimental armoured hose levelling pipe' and though this drawing specifically referred to the 7200 2-8-2Ts, drawing 134289 was subsequently issued in 1954 to make the new arrangement a full modification to be ultimately fitted to all the 2-8-0 and 2-8-2Ts. This observation soon appeared in *The Railway Observer: The cast-iron water equalising pipes connecting bunker and side tanks on the 2-8-0Ts are being replaced by fabricated elbow pipes joined by thick india-rubber hoses. 4276, 5206 and 5244 have been altered together with 2-8-2T 7225.* The pipes were altered at Swindon – see resplendent 4270 for instance, *sans* levelling pipe in June 1954. C. Leigh-Jones, ColourRail

4266 comes east through Cardiff General with some mysterious-looking loads, 4 October 1957. J.T. Rendell, transporttreasury

4266 at Swansea East Dock on 8 September 1951. In contrast to 4261 in the same period for instance, at Llantrisant, it has had the large first emblem applied. A long fire disposal shovel is perched on the tank top. H.C. Casserley, courtesy R.M. Casserley.

Back home, 4289 on the 'firepit' at Severn Tunnel Junction. A.E. Elias, transporttreasury

DUST AND ASHES

4292 serves to illustrate perfectly the 'home life' of the eight-coupled tanks, though it is worth noting that when out at work, they were as often as not rolling through wooded valleys and amid glorious moorland. Here is our 4292 on the fire roads at Neath MPD in March 1963, with the attractive matching stonework of shed and coal stage. I. MacKenzie, transporttreasury

4292 back in the queue on the Neath firepit, on 23 March 1963. The rails on which the ash wagon is standing have all but disappeared! RailOnline

5255 Newport Ebbw Jct 5/1/26; Aberbeeg 21/3/26; Newport Ebbw Jct 18/4/26; Aberbeeg 10/7/27; Newport Ebbw Jct 7/8/27; Aberdare 1/9/29; **Rebuilt as 7220 17/9/35**

5256 Newport Ebbw Jct 4/1/26; Cardiff Canton 21/2/26; Severn Tunnel Jct 28/11/26; Cardiff Canton 26/12/26; Aberdare 12/5/29; **Rebuilt as 7221 25/9/35**

5257 Cardiff Canton 6/1/26; Cathays 7/5/32; Cardiff Canton 4/6/32; **Rebuilt as 7222 18/10/35**

5258 Neath 9/1/26; Landore 1/9/29; Duffryn Yard 19/11/32; **Rebuilt as 7223 10/10/35**

5259 Newport Ebbw Jct 13/1/26; Cathays 2/7/32; Newport Ebbw Jct 30/7/32; **Rebuilt as 7224 2/11/35**

5260 Newport Ebbw Jct 11/3/26; Aberbeeg 7/7/29; Newport Ebbw Jct 4/8/29; **Rebuilt as 7225 28/10/35**

5261 Newport Dock Street 10/3/26; Newport Pill 14/4/29; Newport Ebbw Jct 21/11/31; **Rebuilt as 7226 23/11/35**

5262 Swansea East Dock 16/3/26; **Rebuilt as 7227 27/11/35**

5263 Neath 19/3/26; Llanelly 12/3/32; Pantyffynon 10/3/34; Llanelly 22/9/34; Neath 12/1/35; **Rebuilt as 7228 14/12/35**

5264 Cardiff Canton 25/3/26; Cathays 13/4/30; **Rebuilt as 7229 24/8/35**

5265 Cardiff Canton 23/3/26; Cathays 2/10/27; Barry 4/.6/32; Llanelly 1933; **Rebuilt as 7230 13/12/35**

5266 Newport Ebbw Jct 31/3/26; Llanelly 20/3/27; Newport Pill 10/5/30; Newport Ebbw Jct 17/11/34; **Rebuilt as 7231 14/12/35**

5267 Newport Ebbw Jct 27/3/26; Aberbeeg 3/10/26; Newport Ebbw Jct 20/3/27; Aberbeeg 5/8/28; Newport Ebbw Jct 28/10/28; Aberbeeg 18/1/30; Newport Ebbw Jct 15/12/30; Pontypool Road 10/3/34; Newport Ebbw Jct 7/4/34; **Rebuilt as 7232 28/8/35**

5268 Duffryn Yard 12/4/26; Llanelly 12/5/29; Neath 1933; **Rebuilt as 7233 5/9/35**

5269 Duffryn Yard 9/4/26; Neath 8/7/28; Swansea East Dock 29/8/31; **Rebuilt as 7234 7/9/35**

5270 Landore 14/4/26; Llanelly 24/11/29; Carmarthen 2/8/30; Llanelly 30/8/30; Pantyffynon 6/4/35; Llanelly 24/8/35; **Rebuilt as 7235 1/36**

5271 Aberdare 21/4/26; Cathays 16/11/35; **Rebuilt as 7236 1/36**

5272 Landore 22/4/26; Duffryn Yard 2/8/30; Swansea East Dock 30/8/30; **Rebuilt as 7237 1/36**

5273 Swansea East Dock 27/5/26; Duffryn Yard 10/5/30; Landore 24/10/31; Cardiff Canton 13/1/34; Llantrisant 29/6/35; Cardiff Canton 27/7/35; **Rebuilt as 7238 2/36**

5274 Newport Ebbw Jct 3/5/26; St Blazey 24/11/29; Duffryn Yard 19/11/32; **Rebuilt as 7239 2/36;**

Following put to store when built and until rebuilt as 72XX class
5275 new 7/30; Swindon Stock 1/8/31; **Rebuilt as 7200 30/8/34**
5276 new 8/30; Swindon Stock 1/8/31; **Rebuilt as 7201 31/8/34**
5277 new 8/30; Swindon Stock 1/8/31; **Rebuilt as 7202 5/9/34**
5278 new 8/30; Swindon Stock 1/8/31; **Rebuilt as 7203 11/9/34**
5279 new 8/30; **Rebuilt as 7204 14/9/34**
5280 new 8/30; Caerphilly Works, stored 17/12/32; **Rebuilt as 7205 17/10/34**
5281 new 8/30; **Rebuilt as 7206 18/10/34**
5282 new 8/30; **Rebuilt as 7207 24/10/34**
5283 new 9/30; Caerphilly Works, stored 17/12/32; **Rebuilt as 7208 29/10/34**
5284 new 9/30; Caerphilly Works, stored 17/12/32; **Rebuilt as 7209 6/11/34**
5285 new 9/30; Swindon Stock 26/9/31; Caerphilly Works, stored 17/12/32; **Rebuilt as 7210 1/11/34**
5286 new 9/30; Swindon Stock, 26/9/31; Caerphilly Works, stored 17/12/32; **Rebuilt as 7211 16/11/34**
5287 new 9/30; Swindon Stock 1/8/31; **Rebuilt as 7212 18/9/34**
5288 new 9/30; Swindon Stock 1/8/31; **Rebuilt as 7213 24/9/34**
5289 new 10/30; **Rebuilt as 7214 24/9/34;**
5290 new 10/30; Caerphilly Works, stored 17/12/32; **Rebuilt as 7215 16/11/34**
5291 new 10/30; **Rebuilt as 7216 23/11/34**
5292 new 10/30; Swindon Stock 26/9/31; **Rebuilt as 7217 28/9/34**
5293 new 10/30; Swindon Stock 26/9/31; Caerphilly Works, stored 17/12/32; **Rebuilt as 7218 30/11/34;**
5294 new 10/30; Swindon Stock 1/8/31; **Rebuilt as 7219 10/10/34**
Above information not fully available as 1933 GWR allocation book missing

Following built in 1940
5255 Newport Ebbw Jct 2/40; Barry 9/43; Newport Ebbw Jct 10/8/46; **w/d 24/5/63; mileage 401,689; sold to J Cashmore, Newport 18/9/63**

5256 Newport Ebbw Jct 2/40; Newport Pill 11/42; Newport Ebbw Jct 2/43; Tondu 18/5/46; Newport Ebbw Jct 5/10/46; Newport Pill 31/10/59; Newport Ebbw Jct 11/7/63; Severn Tunnel Jct 5/9/63; Aberdare 27/1/64; Newport Ebbw Jct 6/3/65; **w/d 19/3/65; mileage 385,264 as at 28/12/63; sold to R S Hayes, Bridgend 4/5/65**

5257 Duffryn Yard 2/40; Newport Pill 8/9/56; Aberbeeg 5/9/59; Newport Ebbw Jct 17/6/61; Duffryn Yard 24/2/62; Neath 28/11/63; **w/d 10/64; mileage 384,959 as at 28/12/63**

5258 Aberdare 3/40; **w/d 19/12/62; mileage 449,343; sold to R S Hayes, Bridgend 26/8/63**

5259 Aberdare 3/40; Aberbeeg 17/5/47; Newport Ebbw Jct 24/1/48; **w/d 12/3/64; mileage 421,621 as at 28/12/63; sold to Birds, Risca 23/4/64**

5260 Duffryn Yard 3/40; Newport Pill 12/6/48; Newport Ebbw Jct 17/5/52; Severn Tunnel Jct 11/8/56; Cardiff Canton 14/6/58; Llanelly 9/9/61; Aberbeeg 1/12/62**; w/d 22/3/63; mileage 391,698; sold to J Cashmore, Newport 18/9/63**

5261 Llanelly 3/40; Pantyffynon 5/40; Llanelly 6/41; Pantyffynon 8/41; Llanelly 12/44; Pantyffynon 13/7/46; Llanelly 22/3/47; **Newport Ebbw Jct 2/11/57; Llanelly 30/1/57;** Cardiff Canton 27/12/58; Cardiff East Dock 8/9/62; **w/d 19/3/65; mileage 454,503 as at 28/12/63; sold to R S Hayes, Bridgend 4/5/65**

5262 Cardiff Canton 3/40; Severn Tunnel Jct 29/11/47; Swansea East Dock 21/4/56; Danygraig 21/3/59; Llanelly 11/7/59; Severn Tunnel Jct 10/9/60; Llanelly 16/5/59; **w/d 29/8/63; mileage 483,030; sold to Coopers Ltd, Swindon 31/12/63**

5263 Aberdare 3/40; **w/d 16/12/63; mileage 457,384; cut up 25/1/64**

5264 Newport Ebbw Jct 3/40; Aberdare 16/6/56; Duffryn Yard 15/6/57; St Blazey 30/1/60; Aberbeeg 13/8/60; Severn Tunnel Jct 13/6/63; Neath 11/7/63; **w/d 9/64; mileage 376,675 as at 28/12/63; cut up no date**

5265-5274 cancelled in 1941

5202 with vans at Newport in the 1960s. The traditional BR van was truly universal in its use; the leading example carries labels indicating the recent carriage of Tunnel Cement, ICI fertiliser and, of all things, *The Radio Times*. New front end fitted August 1953. RailOnline

A true Valleys tank line-up at Aberdare on 25 September 1955; 5218 in front with an 0-6-2T and 2-8-2T behind. E. Bridges, ColourRail

5220 running through Cardiff General with, inevitably, a coal train, during 1958. A PO wooden wagon survives at the head of the train. Someone has been remiss in not stowing the coupling on its buffer beam hook, safely out of the way of the ATC apparatus. Rail Photoprint

5222 at Ebbw Junction, 4 May 1951. H.C. Casserley, courtesy R.M. Casserley.

5222 at Glyn Neath shed in the early 1960s, with another 2-8-0T behind. They stand waiting to bank trains off to the right, up through Pencaedrain tunnel to Rhigos Halt. There they'd uncouple and run back down. The engines were outstationed from Neath. A. Scarsbrook, Initial Photographics.

5238 slogs eastwards on the up through running line, between the two great platforms, 2 (right) and 3, at Cardiff General on 24 November 1960. The station had been greatly extended and improved during the 1930s, in work funded by a Government loan scheme. Such were the traffic flows that loaded coal trains like this ran through in both directions. RailOnline

A remarkably clean 5239 inside its home at Neath on 13 May 1956. Neath was an early GW roundhouse, from the 1870s and not one of Churchward's modern post-1900 buildings – it was much smaller for instance. Fully uprated front end. A.R. Carpenter, transporttreasury

A freight comes through Cardiff General from the west behind 5240 on 10 June 1951; photographer crouching down on platform 3 to the left. The almost-art deco 1930s West box (a mirror to the East box on the opposite side of the line, behind us) in the distance. ColourRail

Llantrisant's very own 5241 tucked away amid the weeds at the rear of the shed, 5 May 1951, an already fading BRITISH RAILWAYS on the tank. H.C. Casserley, courtesy R.M. Casserley.

There is also clear evidence of both Bronze and Iron Age activity along the Trent Valley over the last 6000 years. Indeed, this has more recently been confirmed by excavations in the Middle Bailey of the Castle, when flints dating from about 4,000BC were discovered, though whether they were left by nomadic hunter gatherers or by people who actually settled here, we shall never know.

The eroded face of the rock at Highfields, leaving a large overhanging edge

Three miles to the west of the City centre, at Highfields (R), on the University campus, is an area which has remained undeveloped. Here the exposed rock face is still visible. Over the centuries this escarpment has been cut back by the flood plain of the River Trent. A combination of wind and water has eroded the weaker stratas of rock leaving an overhanging ledge. This could very easily be enlarged into a more substantial cave. One such cave still survives. From here, this escarpment continues due east, running beside what is now Castle Boulevard, it then forms the Castle Rock, and the rock outcrop on which the Lace Market stands, and then on into Sneinton. There, until the 1890s, people were still living in cave houses cut back into this exposed rock face.

For thousands of years people have excavated caves, either for burials, or to make homes in which to live, and in countries such as Spain, Turkey and Tunisia, people still live in cave houses. It is therefore entirely possible that, centuries ago, nomads might have come upon this escarpment of sandstone rock and, using simple tools, set about making shelters for themselves and their animals. These caves would have provided them with warm, dry and secure winter quarters. However, it is very unlikely that these early cave dwellers would have excavated underground caves, i.e. cave cellars. This is for two good reasons; first, there would be no need, and secondly, cave cellars are quite unsuitable to live in. Without proper ventilation the atmosphere soon becomes damp, and the air stale, this is still very apparent in the Drury Hill caves, which are no longer open to the elements.

We know very little about what might have happened to those early people, the Celts, or Ancient Britons. Pits containing pottery from about 100BC have been discovered in the Lace Market, although this probably indicates individual farmsteads rather than a "settlement". There is no evidence of any Roman settlement in Nottingham, though there was a fort three miles to the west, at Broxtowe. Nor do we know if the Celts were still living here before the arrival of the Saxons, in about the 6th Century. They built their new town on what was, possibly by then, a deserted rock plateau (now The Lace Market), building houses of timber and mud. This town known as Snotengeham, soon became a prosperous trading centre, and was protected by a ditch on three sides, and by the rock cliff to the south. Once property boundaries became fixed and space restricted, it is entirely possible that the Saxons might have excavated pits, wells and cellar caves for storage. They might also have taken over, and enlarged, some of the deserted caves that had previously been cut into the rock face.

So what did Asser actually mean when he says that the town was called Tig Guocobauc, in Latin Speluncarum Domus. Was he suggesting that it had been a Celtic settlement of cave dwellers? Or was he simply saying that this was the name the Celts called this place, because of all the caves that may have honeycombed the rock faces?

A few caves, cut into the rock face around the Castle Rock, survive. It is fascinating to think that they might have been cut thousands of years ago, but to do so must depend on speculation rather than hard evidence. What, however, we can be pretty sure about, is that all the cave cellars are of much more recent origin. Some in the Lace Market may have been started during the Saxon period, but the vast majority were excavated after the Norman Conquest in 1066.

2   The Myths

Unfortunately, the Victorians failed to distinguish between the *caves cut into the rock face*, which had by then for the most part disappeared, and the *cave cellars*. They fell into the trap of believing that *all* the caves had been cut at one and the same time. Relying on Asser, they therefore concluded that since the Ancient Britons had called the place Tig Guocobauc, they, or even earlier peoples, must have constructed *all* the caves, *including* the cave cellars.

In 1892 a number of cave cellars were discovered in 'the condemned area', which was being demolished for the construction of King Street, just north of the present Council House (20). Mr Clements, an archaeologist, made a model of a cross-section of these caves, pillars and all. He believed, wrongly, that they were dwellings and not storage caves. So on the surface of the model he drew, not houses, but a back drop of open countryside with trees and prehistoric hunters, who supposedly "inhabited" these caves, "with the idea of representing the state of affairs before the surface was built over". It was rather like drawing a cross-section of London showing the tunnels used by the Underground, and then showing the Roman town above and thereby claiming to prove that the tunnels were constructed by the Romans!

Clement's model of the caves under King St 1892

Nevertheless, Clement's misinterpretation of the truth was very much in vogue, and was to lead some archaeologists to even more fanciful theories. One of the flaws in Clement's interpretation was that prehistoric man did not make brick staircases, so all such entrances to the caves had to be ignored, as being of much more recent origin. How then did prehistoric man enter these great cave cellars? The answer was provided by the wells and pits. Many of the wells have hand holes cut into their sides, either to assist in their construction, or to allow them to be cleaned. These were now seen as entrance shafts to the cave cellars. But why should such a difficult and hazardous entrance be necessary, for it would be rather akin to climbing down your chimney to get to your living room? The answer, the archaeologist concluded, was to protect the entrances, since the ground above was inhabited by wild and ferocious beasts!

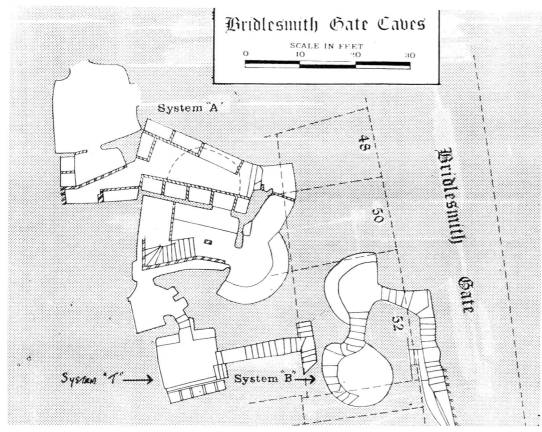

Bridlesmith Gate Caves

SCALE IN FEET

System 'A'

System "I" →   System 'B' →

Plan of Bridlesmith Gate Caves. (R. Sheldon)

The only cleared stairway leads first through a small cave which was probably used for storage and then to the Domed Cave. Prior to 1976 this cave was filled with 18th and 19th Century rubbish. It was cleared by members of NHAS to reveal one of the deepest caves yet discovered. From the entrance it has a circular stone stairway with rough cut steps leading down the side to its base. It is $4^{1}/_{2}$ metres from base to roof and this depth and its shape suggest that it was probably constructed as an icehouse. Ice would be brought into the cave in the winter from the nearby rivers and pools. It would be stored in layers separated by straw and then sold to the population during the hot summer months.

From a shop cellar above is another set of steps leading to a rectangular cave - the Apothecary's Cave - which has an 18th Century brick cupboard. This was probably used to store either wine or chemicals, in connection with the druggist business of the Cox or Cocks families, who owned the house above. A small hole connects with a second system of caves, known as System A, which underlies the adjoining properties - numbers 48 to 50. This was clearly made by accident. One can imagine property owners expanding their businesses by enlarging their caves, until suddenly they break through to

Lucy Lockett and other members of NHAS, examine the newly cleared Domed Cave in 1978, note on the right, the rough steps down. (NHAS)

their neighbour's cellar. If the hole created was large then the gap would be filled by building a brick wall. Subsequent owners, or archaeologists, might then remove the walls creating a cave complex, where none originally existed before.

Only five caves in System A have been excavated. One of them contained a fire pit filled with shards of pottery and part of a quern (used to grind corn) of about 1300. Another cave was, until recently, lined with 18th century brick wine bins. These have been removed in part to expose a large roughly hewn pit about 1.5m deep in the floor of the cave. It was originally thought that this may have been an unfinished malt kiln, but there is no stoke hole, so this may well be simply an unfinished cave.

Rock steps leading to the entrance of the Domed Cave. (NHAS)

*Tours of **Bridlesmith Gate** caves are provided by NHAS., Tel: 0115 926 8568*

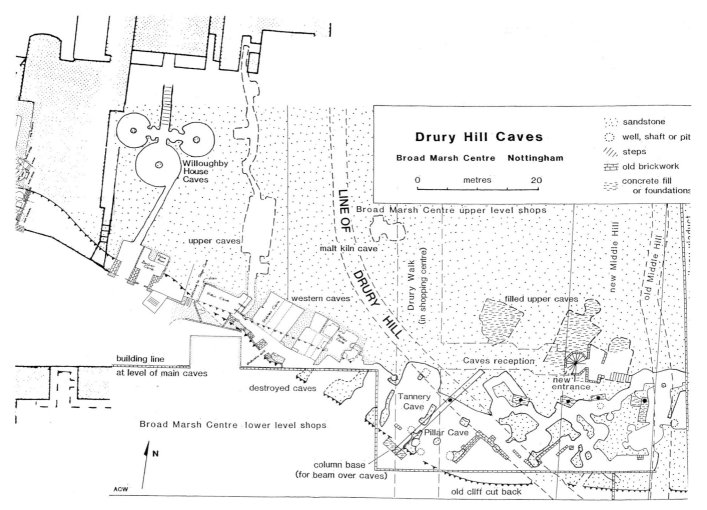

Plan of Drury Hill Caves, note the line of Drury Hill and compare it with the photographs on pages 15 and 17 and the Willoughby caves, top left, see photos on pages 7, 18 and 33. (Sheldon/Waltham)

5   Nottingham Castle

King David's Dungeon (E)

For five hundred years Nottingham Castle was the principal Royal Castle in the Midlands. As such it was not only a fortress and a palace, but a royal prison as well. A new dungeon was constructed "beneath the High Tower" for 'The Scottish prisoners' in 1370. Another was visited by the traveller John Leland in 1540. "We go down" he says, "many steps with a candle lighted into a vault underground, and rooms cut and made out of the very stone, in the walls whereof the story of Christ's passion are engraved, using only his fingernails, by David, King of Scotland, (as they say) who was kept prisoner there." King David was indeed imprisoned here in 1346, though whether, according to another visitor, James Taylor in 1627, he "languished" in such a cave cell for "eleven long years" seems doubtful.

In 1651 the Royal Castle was slighted, and in due course the ruins were acquired by the Duke of Newcastle. He built the present Ducal Palace in 1679. One of his successors, in 1720, undertook the first excavation at the Castle, searching in vain for what was then called **'Davy Scot's Hole'** (2). When Charles Deering visited in 1751, he found a blocked up doorway "at the east end of this yard ... this opened the way into ... James Scott's Hole ... His Grace when at Nottingham ... had this place opened, but it being almost entirely filled up with rubbish, no discovery could be made."

King David's Dungeon, showing the Duke's dividing wall, and on the right the two pointed arches.

Not long after, this cave must have been cleared of rubbish. It was then divided with a brick wall, and the first cave was turned into a wine cellar and brick wine bins were constructed for the Duke's finest wines. The first of these two caves is now known as King David's Dungeon, though whether this was where King David was actually imprisoned is open to doubt. Both the wine and the wine bins have now long since gone.

On the left hand wall, as you enter the cave down a flight of stone steps, are two pointed stone arches. These formerly opened to buildings overlooking the inner moat, but they were sealed, when a bake house was constructed beyond, in about 1250. So this cave must predate that work. It may well have been part of the extensive works carried out by Henry II in 1170, when he enclosed the Middle Bailey with a stone wall. It is, therefore, probably one of the earliest surviving rock cellars in the City.

In recent years, archaeologists have removed some of the blocking masonry to investigate the area behind the wall. Also revealed was a drain cut in the rock floor, which leads into the next cave - Romylowe's Cave - named after a Constable of the Castle who built the tower that formerly stood above in the 14th Century. This has a rock cut fireplace and what appears to be a window, now blocked with rubble. From here a further flight of steps leads up, through the surviving Castle walls, to a further cellar directly beneath the Ducal Palace. This too would have been used as a store and later by the Duke of Newcastle as a wine cellar.

Parallel to this cave, though not accessible from it, is the Slaughterhouse Cave used by the Duke of Newcastle to hang and prepare carcasses of animals hunted by him and his guests, in the adjoining Park. A brick lined passageway leads to this cave, but, unfortunately, it is not open to the public.

Mortimer's Hole (A)

Numerous stories abound of secret passages that run under the old Town. A passage was said to connect the Castle to Lenton Priory, another to have gone all the way under the Old Market Square, and so on. Unfortunately it appears that none of these stories are true. Why after all would one need to travel underground? Perhaps to avoid detection, and that is probably why the only true passages are actually at the Castle. In 1919, a passage which ran under the old 1790 Hospital building, in what had been the old Northern Bailey of the Castle, was discovered. However when the hospital site was redeveloped in 2000 no trace of it was found (1).

The middle section of the passage. (AT)

The most famous passageway is undoubtedly Mortimer's Hole. It is 105m long; cut through the rock it leads down from the former Upper Bailey of the Royal Castle to Brewhouse Yard at the base of the Castle Rock, some 38m below. It gets its name from the dramatic events that occurred in 1330. The Queen, Isabella, had taken as her lover Roger Mortimer, Earl of March. Together they had plotted and connived in the death of Edward II in 1327. Since then they had ruled the country, the new King, Edward III, having yet to gain his majority. In October 1330 they came to Nottingham Castle to hold a Parliament. Edward III, who had just reached 18, lodged in the Town. He determined to take his rightful place as king and so entered into a plan to surprise and capture Mortimer. He, with a small band of men, and with the help of the Governor of the Castle, gained access to the Castle through a secret unguarded passage, which contemporary accounts referred to as 'a postern in the park.' Despite being well guarded, the King's supporters avoided detection, and Mortimer was taken by surprise in the Queen's Chamber. He was seized and taken to London where he was later executed.

Other caves were enlarged. There are substantial caves on the north side of Wollaton Street (3). These were again cut into the exposed face of the rock, which meant they could be entered at ground floor level. These were used for making wagons until the end of the 19th Century. A very large and impressive cave 18m x 8m, with six flared rock

The caves under Habitat (Pearsons), the earlier cave with a central pillar may have been a maltings, subsequently it was greatly enlarged. (TW)

columns and elegant roof arching, still survives under what used to be Pearson's Department store on Long Row (6), now Habitat. Another cave on Talbot Street (4) was excavated in 1885 to form a cold store for Burtons the Provisioners. It was cut around an enormous central core of rock which was left to support the cave roof. It was still being used until the 1960's.

A prisoner left to rot in a cave cell under the Shire Hall!

Some caves were closed and replaced with new buildings. In the 1820s a new prison was built behind The Shire Hall (P), in the Lace Market. This replaced the ancient rock cut cells. Luckily some of these survived, including one that may have been used as the prison chapel. They have now been reopened and form part of the Galleries of Justice. There were other dungeons under the old Town Hall, which formerly stood on Weekday Cross. Sadly these were all demolished in 1899, with the construction of the Great Central Railway.

The Galleries of Justice, *open from 10am to 4pm. Tickets can be purchased at the entrance. Tel 0115 988 1956.*
Wollaton Hall: *Tours of the hidden parts of the Hall and the caves at 11.30am and 2.30pm. Tel: 0115 915 3900.*
The Willoughby Caves *by arrangement with the owners, or NHAS, Tel 0115 926 8568.*

8   Victorian Follies

Above; the steps, modelled on Haddon Hall, cut out of the rock, lead down into another cave in which is carved, out of the solid rock, Daniel in the Lions Den. (TW) Below; this photograph shows the cave some years ago, before it was damaged. (NEP)

The Victorians' interest in antiquities led some of the most affluent citizens to recreate historic fantasies. They cut passages linking their houses to parts of their garden - or to cave summer houses, some with pillars cut to resemble temples. Sometimes, as we have seen at the Rock Chapel, they converted historic caves. Those who lived on The Ropewalk, located on the sandstone edge overlooking the bowl of The Park, were especially lucky. Here, in 1838, Alderman Herbert constructed the most dramatic underground stairway passage, based on a staircase at Haddon Hall, from his basement down to his garden on the other side of Park Terrace. This led into a cave grotto, 10m x 6m, in which he had carved, out of the solid rock, the life size statues of Daniel surrounded by six lions. Unfortunately, the weather, vandals and visitors have, over the years, inflicted very substantial damage on the sculptures. They are now watertight and secure under a new house, though they are not open to the public.

Some fifteen years later, only a few hundred yards away, T C Hine, the architect for the Park Estate, began constructing a new route into the Park from Derby Road. This grand entranceway, opened on 11th May 1855, is known as the Park Tunnel (H). It is, in fact, two large tunnels, 75m long and 8m high, more than large enough to let two double-decker buses pass side by side.

THE BRADFORD CITY STORY

The Pain and the Glory

By David Markham
and Lindsay Sutton

breedon **books**
PUBLISHING

First published in Great Britain in 2006 by
The Breedon Books Publishing Company Limited
Breedon House, 3 The Parker Centre, Derby, DE21 4SZ.

Cover images Copyright photograph reproduced courtesy of
the Telegraph & Argus, Bradford

ISBN 1 85983 499 X

Printed and bound by Cromwell Press, Trowbridge, Wiltshire.

CONTENTS

FROM CLOGGIES TO CHAMPIONS

A FOREWORD BY DAVID MARKHAM

IT STARTED out as a trial. Some would say that my 30-plus years of covering Bradford City has been a trial ever since.

But the trying times have been more than compensated by the times of celebration, exhilaration and the sheer fascination of finding out what goes on in front of house, and behind the scenes.

It's true to say that the phone call to the Keighley office of the *Bradford Telegraph & Argus* that day in the early 1970s changed my life. Would I be interested in covering Bradford City on a month's trial basis?

Was it a sentence or an opportunity? It was certainly a challenge. I also think I deserved the chance. After all, I'd stood on a buffet at the Bradford end when I was an eight-year-old lad as Bradford City played Rotherham United in a Third Division North match. We lost 2–1, but I'd stuck with them. They could stand by me now.

That was way back on 2 October 1948, a month before my co-author Lindsay Sutton – known in the trade as 'LRS' – was brought screaming into the world at St Luke's Hospital in the Little Horton end of the city.

His recollections, therefore, begin about a decade on from mine, but he's done his fair share of penance down at Valley Parade. It was just our luck to have to watch City during their 48-year marathon stint in the lower Divisions. We often tell ourselves that it's the hard times that make the good times feel so much better.

'Markham and Sutton' might sound like an old-style music hall act, but our defence is that we were brought up all too often on a comedy of errors that masqueraded as football. The whole scene we witnessed as young supporters at Valley Parade was straight out of a Bill Tidy 'Cloggies' cartoon. A quagmire of a pitch; a crumbling relic of a ground, with one end named after a hill in the Boer War; a steady diet of low Division soccer; a backcloth view over the railway goods yard and the power station cooling towers, topped off by the yellow, nitric acid fumes, which drifted over the ground from the nearby chemical works. Ah, such memories!

I remember one whimsical feature in which my co-author amused us all by recalling his first-ever youthful visit to a ground other than Valley Parade. It was Barnsley, and he wrote that it was the first time he realised that soccer could be played on dry land! For at least seven months of the season, City's pitch resembled the Mississippi delta. As he says,

'You half expected the goalkeeper to be called Tom Sawyer.'

We are both classic Bradford City supporters, both 'Pennine Boys' from what 'LRS' calls 'the hills and mills' end of town. Both of us turned out to be journalists, and both of us came together to pool our resources, initially in recognition of Bradford City's centenary, which my co-author sometimes refers to as The Hundred Years War.

It sometimes felt like it too, yet I savoured the privileged opportunity of reporting on more than 1,500 City matches through all the Divisions, from the old Fourth to the modern-day Premiership, and into Europe.

Our book is not meant to be the absolute definitive 'Statto' book on the club, one which contains every answer to any pub quiz question. We have aimed at producing a readable book, looking at the bigger picture, revealing the stories behind the stories. The stuff Joe Public doesn't always get to know.

We have concentrated on the modern era that is relevant to the current follower of the game. The last five years have been sensational, a roller coaster ride to the Premiership and then twice through the process of administration, when the club's very existence was called into question.

In fact, the story of the modern era, when the club finally broke the 48-year sentence of lower division purgatory, began just 21 years ago. We have talked to every manager and the key figures who played their part in that journey from relative obscurity to the so-called high life. Their stories are colourful, revealing and often controversial. We have aimed at setting records straight and telling it how it is, not how some would want it to be told. Unfettered objectivity has been our aim, not propaganda masquerading as news.

Some things never change in the robust, rough-and-tumble world of professional football. Managers always have reasons why they never quite fulfilled their dreams. Players always point to management or the nasty board. Directors always say how they are misunderstood or under-appreciated.

The game also throws up larger-than-life characters and Bradford City has had more than its fair share. Take Abe Rosenthal, an amateur who played the game for fun, he had two ice cream and lollipop businesses, one near Valley Parade, the other across the Pennines. He transferred himself between City and Tranmere half a dozen times whenever his business requirements demanded it.

Then there was the perma-tanned and permed chairman Bob Martin, whose name naturally gave rise to a thousand 'dog's life' headlines. Talking of splendid names, there was, of course, the one and only Stafford Heginbotham, twice chairman and twice saviour of Bradford City, and described by so many interviewees as an archetypal 'likeable rogue'.

However, no one has caused such controversy, deep feelings and acrimony as City's former chairman Geoffrey Richmond. His impact, over nine recent and eventful years, has been the stuff of TV drama, with critic and supporter battling it out for the final word. At first, he declined to be interviewed, perhaps sensing that we were determined to be objective rather than simply eulogistic, fair rather than fulfilling a PR

goalkeeper who weighed 22 stone! The even more amazing thing is that Fatty Foulke was good.

The Incredible Bulk came from Chelsea with a reputation for being one of the best 'keepers of his era. His clearances were extraordinary, and he could punch the ball further than most outfield players could kick it. Willie Foulke didn't stay long, but his added value was as much for giving the game yet another talking point in Bradford. In marketing terms it was a masterstroke, and the man who pulled it off was manager Peter O'Rourke.

A couple of months into the season, manager Robert Campbell had resigned from his post, and a month later O'Rourke hung up his boots to take over the management role. He had been an example on the pitch and was to prove to be a brilliant manager, who would lead the club to one of its most triumphant achievements a couple of years on.

Perhaps the highlight of the 1905–06 season was the club enjoying the first of what would be many major FA Cup feats. (Even in their darkest hours City have often been able to cheer us up with a spectacular Cup result.) Having seen off Darlington and Barrow, City faced First Division Wolverhampton Wanderers, whom they thrashed 5–0 to earn a third-round tie against high and mighty Everton at Goodison Park. It was so nearly 'shock of the day' as City took the goalless tie into extra-time but lost to a scrambled goal seconds before the end of stoppage time.

The FA was less impressed by a home game incident in which City fans pelted Manchester United fans and the referee with mud at the end of a bad-tempered game, which United won 5–1. Valley Parade was ordered to be closed for two weeks, and the club was ordered to move the dressing rooms, presumably out of the line of fire of angry fans.

City finished in 11th place but had accumulated an overdraft of £1,074 and a trading deficit of more than £2,000. The alarm bells were ringing, just as they were to do on at least three other occasions over the next century. A Commission of Inquiry concluded that a Limited Liability Company should be set up, and, though this was resisted at first, limited company status was adopted two years on.

1906–07

OVER THE years, at the onset of any period of 'financial indigestion', to coin a phrase of future chairman Geoffrey Richmond, the cry of 'amalgamation' went up.

So it was in the 1906–07 season when it was proposed that City merge with Bradford Rugby Club, who played at Park Avenue. The latter couldn't make ends meet playing Rugby League and wanted a slice of City's Association Football success. The dramatic outcome of the meetings, negotiations and divisions that ensued was to be perhaps THE turning point for sport and sporting venues in Bradford.

The facts are these: City's lease for Valley Parade was with the Midland Railway Company and had to be renewed every three months, with no apparent prospect of a long-term deal. It was also the club committee's view that the ground was unfit for First Division crowds, should City make the grade. Across the city in the leafier suburb of Horton was Park Avenue, where cricket had been played since 1836 and rugby since 1880. Perhaps more to the point, there was a 999-year lease on the ground.

Given that the Park Avenue outfit wanted to give up rugby, wouldn't it be logical for the two clubs to pool resources, with City moving to Park Avenue? The latter's ground was more developed and in a much more pleasant area than Valley Parade, which was surrounded by blackened mills, gaunt warehouses, cramped terraces of back-to-back houses, and which clung crazily to the side of a steep and somewhat precipitous valley overlooking the bleak railway sidings below. It could have featured in one of Bill Tidy's 'Cloggies' cartoons or in the *You think you've had it hard* scripts from Michael Palin's Yorkshireman.

But this was no subject matter for jest. The 'hills and mills' boys of Bradford City were wary of the motives of Park Avenue's wealthy patron Harry Briggs. Besides which, they didn't want to give up their spiritual home. The club's officials did talk and appeared convinced that a merger would make sense for both concerns. Perhaps it did make sense on paper, but, as Great Uncle Albert would often say, 'Since when was football played on paper?' At an incredibly well attended meeting of Bradford City members at Westgate Hall, on 28 May 1907 the voting went 1,031 against a merger with 487 in favour.

The idea was as dead as a Dodo. The result also meant a go-it-alone move by the Bradford Rugby Club, who set up a soccer club in their own right, Bradford (Park Avenue) AFC. The rugby fraternity went off in a huff to form Bradford Northern into the bargain.

And so a city whose sporting loyalties were divided between rugby and football would go on to struggle in their endeavours to support two professional football clubs over the next 67 years.

It had all hinged on the decision of one meeting, albeit with 1,500 people present.

Meanwhile, City had been strengthening their squad and their position in Division Two. Yet another Robert Campbell – and another Scotsman to boot – arrived at Valley Parade. He was a full-back from Millwall, and he was joined by fellow defender Fred Farren from Kettering.

The astute manager Peter O'Rourke then signed Frank O'Rourke, no relation whatsoever, who was to become an invaluable goalscorer in City's push for greatness. The bustling Airdrieonians centre-forward had impressed so much in a friendly at Valley Parade that the board agreed he could be signed that very night. The deal was negotiated in the team's hotel after the match, a clear sign of confidence and momentum.

The building blocks were in place, and City ended up in fifth place, just 13 points behind League leaders Nottingham Forest. Hopes were high for the following season.

FATTY FOULKE ARRIVES – City signed legendary 20-stone goalkeeper Willie 'Fatty' Foulke from Chelsea in November 1905. Foulke was a big name signing but not just because of his weight – he was an England international and played in three FA Cup Finals for Sheffield United. A line-up in 1906–07. Back row, left to right: Peter O'Rourke (secretary-manager), James Roberts, Leonard Newton, Willie Foulke, Robert Campbell, Albert Wise, Harry Hanger, Charlie Harper (trainer). Middle, left to right: Willie Clarke, James Millar, Wallace Smith, George Robinson, Albert Bartlett, James Garton, Alec Whaites, Sam Higginson. Front, left to right: James McLean, Fred Farren.

CITY ICONS – Top, left to right: Frank Thompson, Frank O'Rourke, Dickie Bond. Bottom: Bob Torrance.

1914–18

WITH LEAGUE football suspended, players – like everyone else – were enlisted to fight for king and country. In the mass slaughter that followed in the trenches, City lost no fewer than nine players: Bob Torrance, who had served the club so well, the one-and-only Jimmy Spiers, whose goal had brought the FA Cup to Bradford, Evelyn Lintott, something of an intellectual whose personality lit up the dressing room and the field of play, Jimmy Conlin, one of City's first internationals, James Comrie and Gerald Kirk, two decent central-defenders, and three promising reserve players, George Draycott, Ernest Goodwin and Harry Potter. Also, the Germans captured Dickie Bond on the Somme while he served with the Bradford Pals and then paraded him as a celebrity prisoner of war.

1919–20

CITY MAY have got back in business but the spectre of the Great War hung over every community in the land. It was a relief to get back to the way things were, though there were far too many faces missing in the crowd. To be honest, it was another lull before another storm for City.

They had an unremarkable season in the First Division, ending up in 15th place, but did well in the FA Cup before going out at Bristol City in the quarter-final. It was the farthest City would go in the Cup for 56 years. Hard times were ahead.

Their line up had two major changes: the bald-headed Charlie Storer replaced Bob Torrance, who had been killed in action, and Jimmy McIlvenny found a regular place. He had made his debut in 1910–11

as an 18-year-old, but only some time later did he make his mark, scoring 65 goals in 111 wartime matches. Pre-war stalwarts Frank O'Rourke, Robert Campbell and George Robinson had all retired, as had centre-forward Albert Shepherd, who played for just one season after joining City from Newcastle United while George Chaplin left to join Coventry. Robinson became first-team trainer while O'Rourke continued to play for the reserves.

Seven players formed the basis of the team, right-back Fred Potts, an ever present with 42 appearances, Storer and Dickie Bond with 41, goalkeeper Jock Ewart with 40, Joe Hargreaves with 39, McIlvenny with 31 and Oscar Fox with 29. But the team were growing old and it would be City's failure to rejuvenate and rebuild the side that would lead to the demise in the early and mid-1920s.

McIlvenny was top scorer in the League with 13 goals, while Bond scored 11, plus two in the Cup against his old club Preston. Strangely, City did not have a regular centre-forward, with Scot James Marshall, Ernest Goldthorpe and Harold Walden all sharing the role as they tried to find an effective successor to Frank O'Rourke. Marshall was signed just before the war from Partick Thistle but left a month into the 1920–21 season to join Oldham, while 19-year-old Goldthorpe was drafted in from Spurs.

Scottish left-back Alex Doolan gained a regular place in the second half of the season in place of Irvine Boocock, but he left to join Preston at the start of the following campaign after eight years at Valley Parade. Another Scot, George Waddell, who joined City just before the war from Glasgow Rangers, gained a regular place at left-half in the middle of the season, but he also left for Preston at the same time as Doolan. City also played Joe Marsh at inside-right, a signing from junior football at South Kirkby four months into the season, as they tried to ring the changes.

POST WAR LINE-UP – The team that lost 4–1 at West Bromwich Albion in September 1919, the first season after the war. Back, left to right: Joe Hargreaves, Irvine Boocock, Craig Brown, Jock Ewart, Charlie Storer, Fred Potts, Donald Duckett. Front, left to right: Peter Logan, Oscar Fox, James Marshall, Alex McGinn, George Handley.

THE 1920s

ONLY BRADFORD CITY could have a comic on its books. He came in the form of the one and only Harold Walden, who was a music hall act in his spare time. Eventually, after his dozen appearances in the 1920–21 season, he made his exit, stage left, to sign for Arsenal. Presumably, he had his eye on playing to the gallery at the London Palladium! Sadly, City didn't play to the gallery or even to a decent standard.

They finished 15th in each of the first two post-war seasons and ultimately 15 points above rock bottom Bradford Park Avenue, who dropped out of the top flight forever in 1921.

The great Peter O'Rourke quit as manager in June 1921 to be replaced by Hull City manager David Menzies, who knew his way round Valley Parade, having been a reserve player, assistant and trainer with City.

The next season even the continuous presence of Donald Duck (Duckett to be precise) couldn't work any magic into a disastrous campaign. In the expanded Division One, City lost 21, drew 10 and won only 11.

Even so, City had every chance to avoid the dreaded drop since they needed only four or five points from their last five matches. They lost them all and went down to Division Two in second from bottom spot, above another struggling club,

Manchester United. History tells us that the Reds did not have to wait another 77 years to claim their place back in the top flight. Sadly, that was City's fate.

Not surprisingly, some of the older players, notably Dickie Bond and Billy Hibbert, both 38, Oscar Fox, Fred Potts, Jimmy McIlvenny and Irvine Boocock left or retired in a big clearout. Bond didn't want to leave and actually joined Blackburn for another season just to prove a point.

Unfortunately, Menzies could neither prevent relegation nor fashion a team remotely capable of winning back their place in Division One. The new players he brought in were a mere shadow of the former familiar names who had graced the First Division.

Above all, City were chronically short of goals as they finished 15th in the Second Division in 1922–23. The next year it was 18th, and, to make matters worse, Leeds United finished Champions to claim their place in the top Division. It was as if City had settled for mediocrity, which made a mockery of their explosive impact on football during the previous decade. In 1924–25 they finished 16th, just four points above the drop zone, and, after faring no better the following campaign, manager David Menzies resigned after five years in charge. He later managed Doncaster Rovers before going back to Hull.

His successor was an ex-Newcastle

defeat at Valley Parade on Easter Monday was particularly frustrating. City had held their high-flying opponents to a goalless first half only to lose 3–2. It was little consolation that they went down in the second from bottom spot, four points above rock bottom Manchester United but four points adrift of Everton.

The basic problem was that since the war City had been engaged in a vain effort to replace an ageing side and the club spent a small fortune on new players during the 1921–22 season. They used 33 players that season in their failed bid to avoid relegation. Among the newcomers were left-back Billy Watson signed in May 1921 for a club record £3,000 from Scottish club Airdrie. Watson missed only three matches in his first season and was a regular for 10 years, making 347 League and Cup appearances. Centre-half David Pratt from Celtic and inside left Andrew Chalmers from Dumbarton were among those who arrived during the season. Pratt, signed in November 1921, was a regular in his 14 months at Valley Parade, making 55 League and Cup appearances before he was transferred to Liverpool, while Chalmers stayed four years with the club.

The notable departure in the clearout at the end of the season was England international Dickie Bond, who left Valley Parade after 13 splendid years of service. Billy Hibbert, Jimmy McIlvenny, Oscar Fox, Fred Potts and Irvine Boocock were among other departures.

Now the delights of South Shields, Clapton Orient and Port Vale beckoned. On the other hand there was West Ham, Blackpool, The Wednesday (as the Owls were then called) and Leeds United to play. Hope springs eternal to the soccer supporter.

1922–23

MANCHESTER UNITED may have come down with Bradford City the previous season, but the soon-to-be mighty Reds had no intention of staying in Division Two, unlike their Yorkshire counterparts.

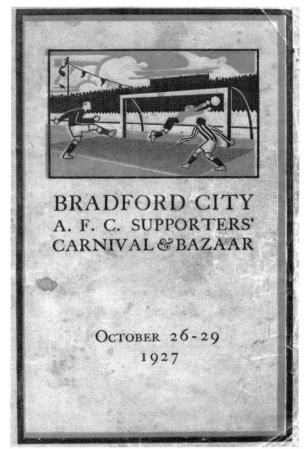

MONEY RAISER – The programme for the supporters' bazaar in 1927 that raised a large amount of money during the club's financial crisis.

The two sides drew 1–1 home and away in the League, and at Valley Parade in the FA Cup first round, although United won in the replay at Old Trafford. By the end of the season United were in fourth place, while City languished in 15th position.

It proved to be the start of five frustrating seasons in Division Two for City. They rang the changes in a vain bid to reclaim their First Division status, but few of the newcomers matched the older players they replaced. City's season had started well as they paraded four new signings and won their first two matches. They then lost their next six without scoring a single goal. Hardly the bounce back to the top flight that everyone had hoped for.

In fact, scoring goals was a huge problem

during the entire season, and City scored only nine in 16 matches to the end of November. With only six wins in 29 matches, by the middle of February there must have been a strong chance that they would be relegated for the second season in a row. However, they then won four in an unbeaten run of six matches and managed to finish safely in that 15th spot.

Close season signing Andrew Cant, another Scotsman, was a particular disappointment. Given the centre-forward berth at the start of the season, Cant began well enough, scoring a goal in each of the first two matches as City beat West Ham and Stockport. But he lost his place and scored only three goals in 13 matches. Not surprisingly, midway through the following season he was on his way back to East Fife.

City scored only 41 goals in 42 League matches, with inside-forward Cecil Kilborn and centre-forward Fred Rhodes the leading scorers with a modest five goals each. Kilborn had joined City as a teenager from Desborough Town in 1919, while 18-year-old Rhodes was signed in December 1922.

STAR MAN – Dickie Bond.

Goalkeeper Jock Ewart was an ever present until the last match when he was replaced by Jim McLaren, signed from Stenhousemuir the previous May. Ewart left the club to return to Airdrieonians at the end of the season. Another notable departure was centre-half David Pratt. He was a big signing when he joined City from Celtic in November 1921 – their last season in the First Division – but was transferred to Liverpool in January 1923.

1923–24

AS CITY bumbled along with no apparent momentum or real ambition, the mantle of greatness was already being passed across the nine-mile gap that separated Bradford from Leeds. City finished 18th out of the 22 teams in Division Two, while Leeds United were crowned Champions and went into the top flight.

The writing looked to be on the wall as City lost at home to the likes of South Shields and Nelson. Still, they beat Barnsley 3–2 and The Wednesday 4–1, although they had no luck in the FA Cup, losing away to Liverpool 2–1.

Once again, goalscoring was a problem. This time they managed only 35, six fewer than their modest tally of 41 the season before, with Fred Rhodes being top scorer with seven. One shining light was the form of goalkeeper Jim McLaren, who was the only ever present, while centre-half Charlie Storer missed only four matches in what turned out to be his last full season of his 11-year career at Valley Parade.

The only other players to top the 30-match mark were dependable left-back Billy Watson and Scottish inside-forward Andrew Chalmers (32) and close season signing from Hull City, the Belfast-born outside-right David McKinney (31). Manager David Menzies again tried to shuffle the pack, using 28 players overall compared with 29 the season before.

Cairns had been an influential figure at Valley Parade, a hard, physical player and a great tactician, although he was nicknamed 'Speedy' because of his lack of pace. City supporters could only marvel as to how good a player he must have been in his prime.

As in the previous season, City made a bad start, winning only three of their first 17 matches, but they then began a spectacular recovery, winning nine, drawing two and losing only one of their next 12 games. They couldn't keep that run of form going to the end of the season, but they did enough to suggest that the following season they could make a significant push for promotion.

Sam Barkas missed part of the season through injury, making 26 League appearances, but Charlie Bicknell was an ever present, while Bobby Bauld played 39 League matches and Harold Peel 35, with stalwart Charlie Moore second leading scorer with 11 League goals in 28 matches.

decisively to solve the goalscoring problem by signing 23-year-old centre-forward Jack Hallows from the Essex junior club Grays Thurrock in November. The tall striker made an immediate impact, scoring 19 goals in an unbroken run of 27 matches as City finished a creditable 10th, eight places better than the previous season. Their best spell was eight wins in the first nine matches in the New Year.

1931–32

JACK HALLOWS, who made his mark in his first season, did even better in his second season at Valley Parade, scoring 21 goals in 34 League appearances as City recovered from a bad start to finish in seventh place.

Most notable newcomer in that campaign was one of the best Bradford-born footballers, Dickie Watmough, who established himself at outside-right after joining City as a 19-year-old amateur in 1931, scoring nine goals in 34 League matches.

As Watmough settled in, City said farewell to Tommy Cairns, whose near five-year career at Valley Parade came to an end. The Scottish international inside-forward had joined City as a 36-year-old in 1927 after a 14-year career with Glasgow Rangers. He was regarded as a short-term signing, but he was not only captain of City's Championship-winning team, he helped them to bed down in the Second Division and did not leave until 1932, by which time he was 41.

1932–33

THE BELIEF that this could be City's promotion year was confirmed as the team won their first five matches, and by the first Saturday of the New Year they were top of the table, leading Tottenham Hotspur by one point.

Clearly, the club had a great chance of going into the First Division and two players were earmarked to strengthen the squad, but the divided board eventually decided against any new signings. It proved to be a bad decision as City slumped in the second half of the season. At one stage they lost eight matches in a row between 21 January and 11 March and finished a disappointing 11th.

Hallows was not as successful as in 1931–32, scoring 12 goals in 37 appearances, and the top scorer was inside-right Stan Alexander with 16 in 37 League appearances. He joined City from Hull City in 1931 and left two years later to join Millwall.

Charlie Bicknell was an ever present for the

second season in a row with 42 League appearances, and centre-half Alf Peachey also played in every match. They were models of consistency, as were Harold Peel with 41 League appearances, Sam Barkas with 40 and Bobby Bauld with 39. But with no team strengthening of note the chance of promotion was gone.

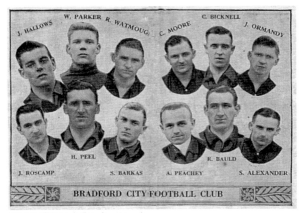

BRADFORD – 1932 squad.

1933–34

ONCE AGAIN City had been short of goals in the previous season and manager Jack Peart rectified this problem by signing the experienced Joe Spence from Manchester United.

Spence, who was then 34, was clearly a short-term signing, but he was an immediate success and scored 23 goals in 41 appearances. He didn't do as well the following campaign and left City to continue his career at Chesterfield in May 1935, having scored 29 goals in 79 League and Cup matches in his two-year spell with the club. He was also a popular player with the supporters and the cry 'give it to Joe' was frequently heard at Valley Parade.

The consistent Jack Hallows supported Spence in the goalscoring stakes, with 17 strikes as City enjoyed their best season since promotion to finish in sixth place in Division Two.

The remarkable Charlie Bicknell completed a proud hat-trick as he played in every match for the third season in row, while Harold Peel, surely one of the finest footballers Bradford had produced, missed only two matches.

It was also the season in which outside-left Jackie Ormandy, who had joined City the previous year, became a regular player. Ormandy, who came from Merseyside, played for Liverpool and Lancashire Boys teams and was an apprentice designer for Prescot Cables.

Peart had spotted him playing for Prescot when he was manager of Rochdale. After becoming City manager, he signed Ormandy on a three-month

1930s SQUAD – By now established as a top-half-of-the-table Second Division club, City's playing staff, directors and officials pose for a photo-call before a pre-season practice match at Valley Parade in 1933–34. Back, left to right: Jack Cliffe, Jack Hallows, Walter Moore, James Clarke, Ken Haigh, Stan Alexander, Walter Bruce, James Collins. Third row, left to right: Geordie Livingston (trainer), Jack Peart (manager), J.R. Gillyard (director), Sam Barkas, Adam Mitchell, Charlie Bicknell, Sam Warhurst, Wilson Parker, Robert Hamilton, Norman James, Charlie McDermott, Tom Robinson (director), Charlie Maley (secretary), Frank Naylor (director), Joe Poole (assistant trainer). Second row, left to right: Tom Power (director), John Driver (chairman), Fred Wallbanks, Dickie Watmough, G. Ebbs, Bobby Bauld, Norman Robson, Harold Peel, Alf Peachey, Charlie Moore, John Roscamp, Hugh McLaren, Bill Burnicle, Frank Obank (director), A.A. McDermott (director). Front, left to right: Jack Ormandy, James Horton, Joe Spence, Tom Barkas.

TRACK RUNNERS – George Hinsley (third left) and George 'Spud' Murphy (far right) are among the City players running round the track in front of the Valley Parade main stand during the 1940s.

Southport, Sunderland and Plymouth player, Matt Middleton was an ever present, while half-back George Hinlsey, one of only a handful of pre-war players in the team, missed only three matches.

Two other pre-war players, centre-forward George 'Spud' Murphy (14) and Alf Whittingham (12), topped the League scoring list.

However, Whittingham, who joined City from an Altofts junior club in 1936, left in the February to join Huddersfield Town, then in the First Division. He scored 24 goals in 87 League matches at Valley Parade, but he was 25 when war broke out, and like many players of his generation he enjoyed his best years during the war when he was one of the most prolific goalscorers in the country.

He scored 20 goals in 36 appearances for City, but it was his extraordinary goalscoring feats as a guest player for Southampton that captured the imagination. He scored 83 goals in three seasons with the Saints, including eight goals in Southampton's 11–0 win in a League South match against Luton in January 1943.

Among the new signings who made their mark was 30-year-old centre-half Lou Bradford from Kilmarnock. He joined City in October 1946 and played in 34 consecutive matches to the end of the season, while full-back Frank Shufflebottom, who later became trainer at Valley Parade, also established himself as a regular in the side after joining City from Nottingham Forest in the same month as Scottish inside-forward Jock Shearer, who arrived from Barker's old club Derby County.

Another player to make his mark that season was Birstall-born half-back Bill Murphy, who joined City from Liverpool in September 1946. He was an amateur at Liverpool, but City offered full professional terms, and he made 149 League and Cup appearances in six seasons at Valley Parade.

This first season after the war coincided with one of the worst winters of the 20th century, and the season proved to be the longest. It began on 31 August, but, in common with other clubs, City were badly hit by postponements, playing only three matches in two months, during February and March, and the season didn't end until 14 June.

1947–48

THIS WAS Jack Milburn's first full season in charge, but it was not a success as the team finished in 14th place. The Second Division seemed a long way off.

ON THE ATTACK – Winger Joe Poole chases a ball down towards the Spion Kop goal during a match at Valley Parade in the late 1940s. Note the old Midland Road stand with the clock.

The team made a good start by winning their first three matches with 'Spud' Murphy and Abe Rosenthal on the mark, but it proved to be a false dawn. Roly-poly built Rosenthal, a skilful but often frustrating inside-forward, had joined City for the first time towards the end of the previous season and was top scorer with 11 League goals in 33 matches, while centre-forward John Neilson, who joined City from Clyde in the October, scored 12 goals, including 10 in the League.

Neilson played with City for only a year, but his Clyde teammate, right-half Andy McGill, who arrived at Valley Parade a month later, made a more significant contribution in his five years at the club.

McGill, who was a natural leader and forceful personality, became captain. As a wing-half, he drove forward to support and instigate attacks and was strong in the tackle and a good distributor of the ball.

Among the departures was 'Spud' Murphy. He left in December 1947 to join Hull City after

making more than 300 peacetime and wartime appearances in his 13 years at Valley Parade. His departure marked the end of an era.

Twenty-seven players were used as Milburn rang the changes and brought in new signings, but the final placing was a big disappointment.

1948–49

WHEN JACK MILBURN stood down as manager, City brought in the experienced David Steele to replace him in July 1948. Steele had a successful playing career as a member of the Huddersfield Town team that won a hat-trick of First Division titles in the 1920s.

He later managed Bradford Park Avenue and Huddersfield Town, but he was working on the family fruit farm when City brought him out of retirement to become their 11th manager in 27 years. Unfortunately, the only fruit he produced in his four-year spell at Valley Parade was a West

ON THE OUTSIDE – The scene in Burlington Street in February 1949 after the gates had been closed for City's match against high-flying Hull City. The match attracted 27,083, the top post-war crowd at Valley Parade, and the gates were closed just before the kick-off with many fans locked out. Some people are seen crowding into the gardens to try to get a view of the match.

Riding Cup triumph against Leeds United in the 1950 Final.

City sunk to new depths in Steele's first season. Despite using a then club record number of 40 players, the team finished bottom of the table and had to seek re-election for the first time in their history as they won only 10 of their 42 matches.

TRAINING – George 'Spud' Murphy (second left) takes part in a 1940s training session with four teammates.

There was only one highlight: a surprising 4–2 win over high-flying Hull City, whose player-manager was the distinguished former England international inside-forward Raich Carter. The match attracted Valley Parade's highest post-war crowd of 27,083, and home fans were delighted to see City beat the Division glamour side with a hat-trick from Scottish centre-forward Jimmy Brown and a goal from Frank Greenhoff, but not even this fine win could inspire the players as they lost eight of their remaining 14 matches.

Brown finished as leading scorer with a modest 11 goals, but he stayed only nine months at Valley Parade. He joined City from Motherwell in November 1948 and before the following season began he was on his way back to Scotland – this time to Queen of the South.

ON THE MARCH – Goalmouth action from City's FA Cup second-round replay against Rochdale during the famous Cup run in the 1959–60 season. Derek Stokes scored both goals in the 2–1 win that set up an attractive third-round home tie against Everton. Stokes scored 10 goals in eight Cup matches that season.

defeat at home to Southampton and finished as leading scorer with a then club record 28 goals in 34 League appearances while scoring six goals in the FA Cup. He ended the season with a flourish, scoring 13 goals in the last 10 matches.

McCole was not only a good finisher but also a skilful player, and the trainer at the time, fellow Scot Jock Robertson, tells how he gave him extra training to match the demands of a faster English game.

It was impossible to keep McCole out of the news, and when goalkeeper Geoff Smith was injured during City's 2–0 win in the third round of the FA Cup at Brighton McCole went in goal and Smith played the rest of the match on the wing. This, of course, was in the days before substitutes.

This win took City into the fourth round where they were beaten 3–2 at Preston. A late goal dashed their hopes of a replay.

1959–60

THIS SEASON will be remembered mainly for a magnificent FA Cup run, which culminated in an epic fifth-round tie against Burnley.

First, though, City suffered a blow when John McCole was transferred to First Division neighbours Leeds United for £10,000 after appearing in only eight matches of the new campaign. There was no obvious explanation for the transfer, but rumour had it that there had been some behind-the-scenes conflict that persuaded Jackson to part suddenly with his prized asset.

However, the manager filled the gap with what proved to be a master stroke when he moved Derek Stokes from left wing to centre-forward, and the move was so successful that he finished the season as top scorer with 25 League goals plus a remarkable 10 goals in City's eight-match Cup run despite missing the last nine matches of the season.

It was a strange season. Before City began their Cup exploits at Barnsley on 14 November the team had won only five of their 19 matches, but Cup progress went hand in hand with improved League form.

During the Cup run City were unbeaten in 11 League matches, winning seven of them and drawing the other four. Once they were out of the Cup, however, they won a mere three of their last 15 matches and ended the season with four successive defeats without scoring a goal. It was

no coincidence that leading scorer Derek Stokes missed the last nine matches through injury. In the Cup, City beat Barnsley 2–1 at home in a first-round replay after a 3–3 draw at Oakwell. They then drew 1–1 at Rochdale in the second round before beating them 2–1 at home, which heralded one of City's best ever Cup triumphs – a comprehensive 3–0 win over Everton in front of 23,550 at Valley Parade. The victory was just as emphatic as the scoreline suggests as goals from David Jackson, John Reid and Derek Stokes knocked the First Division side out of the Cup. City beat Bournemouth 3–1 at home on a wet, slippery pitch in the fourth round to set up one of

CUP ACTION – There was a dramatic climax to the famous City-Burnley fifth-round FA Cup tie in front of a 26,227 crowd in February 1960. City led 2–0 with 15 minutes to go with goals from Bobby Webb and Derek Stokes, but Burnley managed to equalise at 2–2 in the last minute of stoppage time and then won the replay at Turf Moor 5–0. Here, City goalkeeper George Stewart gathers the ball with Malcolm Devitt in support.

last 11 matches, the damage had been done and they missed out on promotion, finishing in fifth place for the third time in seven seasons.

Ian Cooper was the only ever present, but Barry Swallow missed only one match while Pat Liney played 42 matches and John Hall played 40 plus three as substitute. Charlie Rackstraw was leading scorer with 14 League goals, Bannister scored 13 and Aimson, 11. The experienced Jim McAnearney had taken over as caretaker manager following Hair's death, but after City's failure to gain promotion the club decided to look elsewhere for a permanent successor, and McAnearney moved to Rotherham at the end of the season

GO FOR IT – John Hall has a determined look on his face as he sets off on a run.

THAT'S THE WAY TO DO IT – Tony Leighton demonstrates a skill watched by his teammates. Senior players in the picture include Barry Swallow, Archie Taylor, Denis Atkins, Bruce Stowell, Ron Bayliss, Tom Hallett, Charlie Rackstraw, Kenny Wright, Ian Cooper and Peter Middleton.

1968–69

CLEARLY WANTING a fresh start after the disappointment of missing out on promotion, City turned to Reading assistant manager Jim Wheeler as their new boss, and he succeeded where others had failed by leading City to promotion.

Wheeler, who was born in Reading, had spent the whole of his professional career at Elm Park so coming north to Bradford was a brave move.

The new manager made four signings, winger or inside-forward Peter Middleton from Sheffield Wednesday, wing-half Ron Bayliss from his old club Reading, former Park Avenue left-back Gerry Lightowler from Los Angeles Wolves and striker Derek Montgomery from Leeds United, but the only player to claim a regular place was Middleton.

For much of the first half of the season promotion looked a distant prospect, and, after a particularly disappointing 1–0 home defeat against Workington on the last Saturday of December, City were firmly entrenched in the bottom half of the table.

City then transformed their season by embarking on a record unbeaten run of 21 matches. It started with a 2–0 win at Notts County on 11 January and didn't end until City were beaten 2–1 at Brentford in the penultimate match of the season.

At the start of the unbeaten run Wheeler had the good sense to strengthen his squad with what proved to be a shrewd signing.

Norman Corner, who joined City from Lincoln, looked to be a somewhat ungainly character and was not noted for his pace, but he was awkward to mark in the penalty area.

SAFE HANDS – Popular goalkeeper Peter Downsborough.

Edwards strengthened the team by signing midfield player Johnny Johnston from one of his former clubs, Blackpool, during the summer, and then signed another midfield player Ronnie Brown from Plymouth six weeks into the season. A month later he signed his former Bolton teammate, one-time Northern Ireland international John Napier, from Brighton in a £10,000 deal, and he established himself as a regular central-defender.

Scot John Ritchie became the regular goalkeeper, while Bradford-born midfield player Garry Watson made his debut three days before his 17th birthday. City enjoyed a good FA Cup run, reaching the third round when they beat Second Division Blackpool 2–1, with Ingram scoring both goals against his old club. That set up a fourth-round tie at Arsenal, and City were in the game until midway through the second half, until Charlie George broke away to put the result beyond doubt.

Undoubtedly, though, the most important events took place off the field with director Bob Martin taking over as chairman from Stafford Heginbotham in October 1973, while supermarket magnate Ken Morrison joined the board. This ended Heginbotham's eight-year spell as chairman, but he would be back 10 years later to succeed Martin.

1973–74

CITY HAD an improved season without ever threatening promotion and finished in a respectable eighth place. There were two newcomers in the regular starting line-up with Edwards signing another player from Plymouth, midfield player Les Latcham, while striker Bobby Ham returned to City from Rotherham.

More significant signings were also made later in the season. 'Keeper Peter Downsborough joined City from Swindon in a £5,000 deal after an initial loan spell, while the club paid £9,000 to bring former Leeds United and Doncaster Rovers

goals in 40 League matches and one in the FA Cup, while Ingram scored 12 in 37 League matches, including four in a 7–0 win over Darlington just before Christmas and three in the FA Cup. However, the overall performance of the team was disappointing.

Ian Cooper's remarkable consistency continued – an ever present for the third season in a row – while John Hall made 46 appearances. Graham Oates, now established as a defender or midfield player, made 44 and defender David Fretwell established himself as a regular with 42 matches.

BRADFORD CITY

Association Football Club (1908) Limited

Directors:
S. Heginbotham
Chairman

G. D. Ide
Vice-Chairman

P. J. W. Jones
R. Martin
H. B. Metcalfe
E. L. Porter

Hon. Medical Officer:
Dr. R. Strachan

General Manager
and Secretary:
J. Mellor

Team Manager:
G. B. Edwards

**FOOTBALL LEAGUE
DIVISION FOUR**

*Official
Programme*
5p

Saturday 26th August 1972,—Kick-Off 3-0 p.m.

versus

Hereford United

midfield player Rod Johnson to Valley Parade from Rotherham.

The miners strike and the subsequent three-day week in mid-winter meant electricity shortages and, therefore, early kick-offs, plus ground-breaking Sunday matches in the FA Cup. City reached the third round by beating Barnsley 2–1 in a second replay that had a 1.15pm Wednesday afternoon kick-off in December, before meeting non-League Alvechurch in the third round on the first weekend in January. Because some people had to work on Saturdays, the FA gave clubs, including City, permission to play on Sundays.

City beat Alvechurch 4–2 in front of a crowd of 13,062, more than three times the normal League gate, and directors had to man the turnstiles to ease the crowd congestion. City were knocked out in the fourth round, beaten 3–0 at Luton Town

Encouraged by the success of the experiment, City rearranged other League matches to be played on Sundays and gates were higher than average. It was a novel experience, though nowadays, often through the dictation of TV or

1970s SQUAD – City's first-team squad in 1974. Back, left to right: Bobby Kennedy (youth-team coach), Colin Kaye (physiotherapist), John Napier, Ces Podd, Gerry Ingram, Peter Downsborough, Ian Cooper, John Middleton, Joe Cooke, Bryan Edwards (manager). Front, left to right: Ronnie Brown, Rod Johnson, Bobby Ham, Trevor Hockley, Don Hutchins, Garry Watson.

midweek European matches, Sunday matches have become the norm. Gerry Ingram, with 18 League and Cup goals, and Allan Gilliver, with 12, continued their fine striking partnership, while Ham scored 11. John Napier and David Fretwell formed a consistent central-defensive partnership, each missing only two League matches.

1974–75

BY THE mid-1970s Bradford City were settling into no more than a mid-table Fourth Division side, with gates hovering around the 4,000 mark. There were some bold close season moves in the transfer market, but City could finish no higher than 10th.

Manager Bryan Edwards brought back Keighley-born former Welsh international midfield player Trevor Hockey to Valley Parade 13 years after he left City. He re-joined the club from Aston Villa for £12,500, but the move was not a success. Injuries restricted Hockey to 24 appearances, and he left City for the last time the following season.

Edwards also sold Allan Gilliver to Stockport, despite the fact that the striker had scored 30 League goals in two seasons at Valley Parade, but brought in left-winger Don Hutchins from Blackburn in part exchange for Graham Oates. The midfielder or defender went on to have a good career with Blackburn and Newcastle before going to play in the USA.

Hutchins, who played with Plymouth at the same time as Edwards was assistant manager, was a classical winger, sadly a rare species in the modern game, with the skill to beat opponents and the ability to supply crosses as well as scoring goals, and he made 43 League appearances with five goals in his first season at Valley Parade.

City were nicely placed in the top half of the table by mid-January when the directors sprang a surprise by sacking Edwards on a split vote, appointing youth-team coach Bobby Kennedy as manager.

Kennedy, who had played for Kilmarnock and

Manchester City before becoming player-manager of Grimsby, sought to give the team a sharper edge with the emphasis on working harder in training and in matches, but there was no obvious improvement in results as City finished mid-table.

Finances dictated that City operated with a small squad so there was a settled side for much of the campaign, as illustrated by the end-of-season statistics. Peter Downsborough was the only ever present, but Podd played 44 games, Hutchins and Ham, 43, Fretwell and Johnson, 42 and Rod Johnson, 38.

Ham was top scorer with 14 League goals, forming a good partnership with Ingram, who scored 11. Strangely, Kennedy released Ham on a free transfer at the end of the season along with Ronnie Brown, who did not fit in with his plans.

1975–76

THE SEASON was dominated by City's best FA Cup run for 56 years as they reached the quarter-final for the first time since their First Division days in 1920. They were the only Fourth Division side to reach the last eight.

They lost 1–0 at home to Southampton, who went on to win the trophy after beating Manchester United in the Wembley Final. It was a remarkable achievement for City, whose League form continued to disappoint.

The Cup run began with a 1–0 home win over Chesterfield, and they then overcame two tricky away ties, 3–0 at Rotherham in the second round and 2–1 at Shrewsbury in the third. They were then handed a home tie against non-League Tooting and Mitcham who they beat 3–1. That victory set up a difficult tie at Norwich City, then a good-class First Division club. The match was delayed for nine days because of a flu epidemic in Bradford and was eventually played on a Monday evening.

Some outstanding defensive work was needed to keep out the talented Norwich side, spearheaded by Ted MacDougal. Then City shook

Bradford-born David Jackson, who had been released by Manchester United, and then 2–1 at home to Hereford. But they won only two of their next nine matches, and manager John Napier resigned in the October.

City's top target as his replacement was Bolton assistant manager George Mulhall, a personal friend of chairman Bob Martin. He took a lot of persuading to leave First Division Bolton after he and Ian Greaves had led them to the Second Division Championship only six months before, but eventually he joined City in the November.

City won five matches in a row up to Christmas, but there was patchy form in the second half of the season, including five defeats in a row during a crowded April programme when they played 10 matches in 26 days.

A big mid-season transfer deal took Joe Cooke to Peterborough in part exchange for experienced midfield player Lammie Robertson. City also gave a debut to defender Peter Jackson, a few weeks short of his 18th birthday, when he signed as a full-time professional. Jackson, who made nine appearances that season, became a significant player in the years to follow.

David McNiven was top scorer with 15 goals in 43 League matches as City finished a disappointing 15th. Terry Dolan scored a valuable 10 goals from midfield in 40 League matches, while defender Steve Baines scored 10 in 43 matches.

1979–80

CITY GOT off to a flying start as they topped the table after barely a month of the new season, and they showed they meant business when manager George Mulhall took a gamble on signing 'bad boy' Bobby Campbell in December. It was to prove a master-stroke, and ultimately his regular 20-plus goals a season would help ignite City's take-off.

But back to the beginning of the season when City won seven of their first eight matches to establish themselves as promotion candidates, their good form continuing throughout the season with only the occasional blip.

The club had said farewell to two senior players: Rod Johnson, who was given a free, and 'keeper Peter Downsborough, who decided to retire. Sadly, his testimonial match against Huddersfield Town two weeks after the season ended was badly supported. Only 1,200 turned up to pay tribute to one of City's best goalkeepers, even though he wasn't fit enough to play. Who

MIDFIELD PLAYER – Terry Dolan.

VALLEY SCENE – View of Valley Parade towards Midland Road with the Valley Road power station in the background.

HIGH HOPES – City, who were relegated in 1977–78, had high hopes of going straight back to the Third Division but just missed out. Note a new, predominately white kit. Back, left to right: Lammie Robertson, Peter Jackson, Andy Burton, Steve Smith, Mick Wood, Barry Gallagher, Paul Reaney. Middle, left to right: Steve Baines, Terry Cooper, Garry Watson, Don Hutchins, Ces Podd, Terry Dolan. Front, left to right: Keith Bailey, Mick Bates, David McNiven, Hughie Martinez, David Staniforth.

could forget the sad sight of him hobbling round the Valley Parade touchline thanking the few supporters who turned up?

The two important close season signings were centre-forward David Staniforth from Bristol Rovers and defender Terry Cooper from Lincoln. Mulhall, an apostle of possession football, was keen for City to play the ball out of defence as the First Division sides did and Cooper was a key part of this style of football, although Peter Jackson took over from him towards the end of the season.

Steve Smith, who had joined City from Birmingham two seasons earlier, took over from Downsborough and was the only ever present, although Steve Baines missed only one match, as did David McNiven, who was leading scorer for the second season in a row with 17 League goals

and one in the FA Cup. Terry Dolan also had another good season with nine goals in the League plus three in Cup matches. Six of the penalty king's 12 goals were from the spot.

Staniforth began at centre-forward and scored 11 League goals plus one in the Football League Cup, but later moved into midfield once City made their best-ever signing. His name was Bobby Campbell.

The former Northern Ireland youth international and Huddersfield Town player had been sacked by Halifax Town at the end of the previous season for being caught drinking the night before a match. He had spent some time playing in Australia but arrived back in England just before the end of the year looking for a club.

Mulhall, who knew about Campbell's past – he had been banned by the Northern Ireland FA for misconduct on a youth tour – signed him, originally on a month's trial. However, he did so well that City quickly offered him a contract because other clubs were keen to sign him. He scored eight goals in 21 appearances and quickly established a good partnership with McNiven, though the best was yet to come.

Unfortunately, the season that promised so much ended in bitter disappointment. City needed only to draw in their last match at Peterborough to make sure of fourth place, but strangely the players failed to deliver. Peterborough won 1–0 in a drab, lifeless game and no fewer than four other results went against them as they finished in fifth place, missing out on promotion on goal difference.

City played one unusual FA Cup tie in November. They were drawn away to County Durham side Brandon United in the first round, but the FA ruled that Brandon's ground was not up to standard and so the match was switched to Spennymoor United's ground five miles away, where City won 3–0. They beat Darlington 1–0 away in the second round before going out 3–2 in the third round at Carlisle, after leading 2–1 until the closing stages. They were knocked out of the League Cup by QPR, who included former West Ham manager Glenn Roeder in their side.

LONG SERVICE – Defender Ian Cooper, who played 493 League and Cup matches for City – the second highest in the club's history.

'We built up a good camaraderie in the team very quickly. We didn't chop and change the team around a lot. It had to be a family affair. Players respond to that and it creates a good spirit. We used to stop for a drink on the way home from away matches so we were all together – a couple of drinks and we were back on the coach.

'We had a bit of an indifferent start, but then we won nine matches in a row to equal a club record and that got us going.'

Sheffield United brought the run to an end when they beat City 2–0 at Valley Parade on the penultimate Saturday in October and ultimately pipped them for the Championship when they finished top with 96 points with City second on 91.

McFarland said 'Sheffield United were a very strong team and they outplayed us in the home game, but when we played them at Bramall Lane I felt we had matured over the season. We drew 1–1 in front a crowd of more than 24,000, Barry Gallagher equalised from the penalty spot and we held them quite comfortably. The players believed we could get out of that Division.

'I remember our last home game against Bournemouth when we needed one point to make sure of promotion. We were losing 2–1 with a minute to go when Bobby Campbell scored an equaliser in the last few seconds. We went on the balcony to celebrate in front of the fans. I had done that before after winning Championships with Derby. There was heart-warming feeling and

a feel-good factor about everything. We finished off the season in style with a comfortable 2–0 win at Mansfield.

'I remember giving Stuart McCall his League debut against Reading in the first match of the following season – our first in the Third Division. He looked an absolute certainty to become a good player. He was so enthusiastic. We only had two apprentices, but, whereas the other lad fell away, Stuart was a delight to work with. He played in midfield, and he dominated. He used to try to get forward, get on the end of crosses and then get back to defend. I am delighted he has had such a great career.

'You have got to play with enthusiasm. Stuart wanted to win – his attitude was tremendous. There was no doubt he was going to have a good career in the game. He had the advantage of having his father behind him. Andy had been a professional, and he was very supportive of Stuart. I remember that when we trained we used Stuart as a linesman, but we brought him on when someone was injured.'

It was all so promising, with things going so well for Super Mac and for Bradford City. They were 12th in the League and facing Manchester United in their Cup replay when he suddenly left in late November. It may have been too big an offer to turn down, too emotional a pull to fight off. That said, McFarland, now manager at Chesterfield, is big enough to admit it was a wrong move and one he regrets immensely.

1982–83

EVERYTHING LOOKED rosier in the Valley Parade garden at the start of the season following promotion. Experienced player-manager Roy McFarland was all set to lead by example in the higher Division at the age of 34, and he had strengthened the team.

As well as being the inspirational hub of the

promotion side the season before, McFarland had signed former City centre-half Joe Cooke from Exeter and former Barnsley midfield player Mike Lester, also from Exeter, during the season. In the close season in came Stoke goalkeeper Eric McManus and midfield players, the lanky left-sided player Ian Mellor, known as spider, from Sheffield Wednesday, former Huddersfield Town man Terry Gray from Southend and 18-year-old right-back Greg Abbott on a free transfer from

FANS ON THE MARCH – supporters line up outside the old main stand at Valley Parade ready for a march as part of their efforts to save the club during the 1983 financial crisis.

Coventry to begin a nine-year career at Valley Parade. McFarland, with 28 England caps and two League Championships under his belt, knew he needed better quality players, and he had no wish for consolidation.

As well as the new signings, 18-year-old Stuart McCall also made his debt in the opening match of the season – a 3–2 home win over Reading – after two years as an apprentice to mark the start of a long and distinguished career. He played his first three matches at right-back, but by midway through the season he had settled into his natural midfield role.

There was no hint of the shocks to come as City were among the early pacesetters, winning four of their first six matches. Leading scorer from the promotion season Bobby Campbell began the new campaign in great form, scoring eight goals in the first nine League matches with two more goals in the 3–0 aggregate victory over Mansfield in the two-leg first round of the League Cup.

City suffered a dip in form during October but had recovered well in November when the club suffered a body blow. They beat Oxford at home and Brentford away before they faced Manchester United in the third round of the League Cup at Valley Parade. A packed crowd of 15,568 saw the defence, superbly marshalled by McFarland, inspire City to a goalless draw and a lucrative replay at Old Trafford.

Little did they know that by the time the replay would take place later in the month McFarland and assistant Mick Jones would be gone.

McFarland's last match in City's colours was a first round FA Cup tie at Port Vale where a goal from Bobby Campbell gave the Bantams a creditable 1–0 win. It was a happy party that returned to Bradford from the Potteries that Saturday night, but the following lunchtime McFarland and Jones handed in their resignations and 48 hours later they were named as part of Brian Clough's former assistant Peter Taylor's management team at their old club Derby County.

There was anger and shock among club officials

and supporters. Allegations of illegal approaches and poaching were made and they stuck too. Eventually, Derby were fined £55,000 for breaching League rules as well as having to pay compensation to sinned against Bradford City.

City fans felt they had seen a re-enactment of Julius Caesar, the feeling of back stabbing being heightened by the fact that, for once, they felt the club were on their way up following promotion. The fact that McFarland has now revealed he made a mistake is of little consolation.

Caretaker manager Bryan Edwards and chief scout Maurice Lindley were in charge for the League replay at Old Trafford three days after McFarland's departure and City went down to a 4–1 defeat.

They were not long without a new manager, however, for every proverbial cloud has a silver lining. His name was England international defender Trevor Cherry, who was tempted away from Leeds United by City chairman Bob

Martin. Because of his long service at Elland Road, Leeds gave Cherry away for a knockdown £10,000. Even this appeared too much for the cash-strapped club, who had not paid it in full eight months later. It was to prove costly since it was Leeds, demanding payment, who issued the fateful winding-up notice on City on 22 June 1983. Cherry and his able assistant, former Leeds teammate Terry Yorath, were about to get a taste of what managing Bradford City was really like.

Cherry watched his new side draw 1–1 in an FA Cup first-round tie at Mansfield before they won the replay 3–2, but he had to wait two months for his first League win, City ending a run of 12 matches without a win by beating Bristol Rovers 2–0 at home with goals from Campbell and David McNiven on 12 February. However, the match nearly didn't take place at all because one of the Valley Parade floodlights blew down 36 hours before kick-off. The broken pylon had to be made

BACK IN THE THIRD – City's squad are ready for the new season after gaining promotion from the Third Division. Back, left to right: Steve Watson, Barry Gallagher, Ces Podd, Peter Jackson, Ian Mellor, Bobby Campbell, Joe Cooke, John Black. Middle, left to right: Mick Jones (assistant manager), Stuart McCall, Mark Ellis, Garry Watson, Eric McManus, Mike Lester, Dave Hill, David McNiven, Bryan Edwards (physiotherapist). Front, left to right: Terry Gray, John Garside (director), Roy McFarland (player-manager), Bob Martin (chairman), Eddie Sutcliffe, Terry Newman (secretary), Les Chapman. On the ground, left to right: Tony Clegg, Nigel Chippendale.

WELCOME – Chairman Bob Martin welcomes new manager Trevor Cherry in December 1982.

safe before the match could go ahead, and the home match against Cardiff the following Wednesday had an afternoon instead of an evening kick-off, City winning their second match in a row 4–2. The Bristol Rovers match proved to be McNiven's last for City. Soon afterwards he was transferred to Blackpool after scoring 66 goals in 245 League and Cup appearances during five years at Valley Parade.

City ended their eventful season in 12th place and completed their programme with morale boosting home wins over Yorkshire rivals Sheffield United and Huddersfield Town. Once again they owed much to Campbell, who scored 25 goals in 40 League matches and five in Cup games, while left-back Les Chapman was the only ever present. Cherry also showed his willingness to play as well as manage and didn't miss a single League match

after making his debut at Christmas as he made 28 appearances.

Soon, though, football was to take a back seat as financial problems that had been all too apparent at Valley Parade during the season threatened the future of the club during an anxious and eventful summer. The storm clouds may have blown down a floodlight pylon in February, but, more menacingly, the lights were nearly to go out on a permanent basis.

1983–84

THE GAME was very nearly all up. City had had their financial Doomsday dramas before, but this one was the mother of them all. Or so we thought, we were yet to experience the traumatic aftermath of the reign of Geoffrey Richmond. The Bradford public had seen Bradford Park Avenue go down the plug hole. Were City now to follow? The tale is becoming common place nowadays. Small clubs owing huge amounts to the Inland Revenue; players' wages remaining unpaid; the bank saying 'No more!' and directors unwilling or unable to dip into their own pockets to bale out their languishing clubs. City were always a trendsetter, they did it early in the summer of 1983. Thank goodness Trevor Cherry's mum had insisted on him training as a bookkeeper! It came in handy.

The long and short of it is that the club were placed in receivership. As is usual in these cases, supporters rallied round, a public subscription set up by supporter Bill McGrath raised £53,000, including an anonymous £10,000 donation. It all looked doomed to failure when the High Court ordered the club to be wound up… but a new company was formed called Bradford City (1983) Limited, and in the last second of the last minute of the added on period to extra-time the saviours pulled it off. Former chairman Stafford Heginbotham and ex-director Jack Tordoff came together to save the club, with Heginbotham returning as chairman 10 years after he resigned from the board. Their rescue deal was accepted three weeks before the League programme began, and the club were saved … until the next time.

City began the season without Bobby Campbell, he was sold by receiver Peter Flesher to Derby for £70,000 during the summer to raise some much needed cash. Ironically, Derby then fell from financial grace and Campbell came back for about half his outgoing fee in the November and teamed up with new signing, former Leeds United striker, John Hawley, signed as a replacement at the start of the season. Despite the acute financial position, Cherry was also able to sign two 20-year-olds: left-back Chris With from Newcastle and winger Garry Haire from North League club Whitley Bay.

Hawley proved to be a reliable finisher and ended the season with 22 League goals as City finished a creditable seventh after a dreadful start to the season. They failed to score in their first 12 League matches, and by mid-November they were next to the bottom after winning only one of their first 15 League matches – a 1–0 victory at Port Vale in September. Stafford Heginbotham and Jack Tordoff must have despaired as gates dipped below the 3,000 mark following this bad start to the season. The revival started during a home match against Millwall on Saturday 12 November. At 3–0 down with half an hour to play, City were heading for their 10th defeat of the season, but they staged a dramatic comeback with goals from Stuart McCall, Garry Haire and Hawley, enabling them to salvage a 3–3 draw.

That result sparked a remarkable upturn in City's fortunes as they won their next ** matches, scoring 36 goals in the process to set a new club record – the previous record of nine consecutive wins was set in 1954. The run began with a 4–1 win at Brentford and continued with victories against Plymouth (home), Bournemouth (home), Burnley (away), Wigan (home), Lincoln (away), Preston (home), Wimbledon (home), Orient (home) and Exeter (away). It ended with a 2–2 draw at home to Port Vale on 11 February, but by then the ever-enterprising Stafford Heginbotham had organised a celebration dinner at a city centre hotel and that was held three weeks later – a 500-plus sell-out.

Understandably, City could not keep up the momentum of that winning run, but three wins in five days at Easter ensured they finished in seventh place and, after winning only one match in the first 15 matches, they suffered only six defeats in the remaining 31. That sort of form gave them confidence for their successful promotion challenge the following season.

After the floodlight collapse of the previous season, two new pylons were put up and by then it was found that a third would need to be replaced. Once again, the season had no night matches and early kick-offs, but at least the lights were there. They had come perilously close to being turned off forever.

HOW CITY WERE SAVED FROM GOING BUST

JUST 20 years ago an all-too-familiar series of events unfolded that threatened the very existence of Bradford City. For two long, hot summer months of 1983 the club's future hung in the balance.

The brains behind it all was a patient and inventive Bradford accountant Peter Flesher, working alongside solicitor Stephen Gale. They not only masterminded the club's survival after crippling debts of £400,000 threatened to send it under, but Flesher also later joined the board.

It was Flesher and Gale who came up with the brilliant idea that saved the day, saved the club and which he describes as being 'unusual, slightly dubious, but not illegal.'

Their 'brilliant idea' was for Bradford Council to lend Bradford City £100 then ask for it back. City refused, saying they had no money to pay up. The Council could then appoint a receiver, who would then find a buyer. It was novel thinking. It made novel reading, but it did the trick. Without it, Bradford City would have gone under.

Nowadays, everyone is blasé about clubs in crisis. Back then it was a new and frightening experience, and Flesher is in no doubt that under the rules that existed then it was touch and go whether City would survive as a League club.

More recently, in 2002 and again in 2004, City once again faced oblivion, with potential debts of £36 million. Again, the club survived by going into administration, and then coming out of the process with a lot of help from the Rhodes and the Gibb families, plus a helping hand from the Professional Footballers' Association.

Back in 1983, there was no option of going into administration. As Peter Flesher recalls 'In those days the administration process didn't exist. A company had only two choices. Either it went into liquidation or receivership. Liquidation was the end because if you went down that route you lost your Football League registration and the players' contracts went back to the League.

'But the only way you could go into receivership was if the there was a debenture over the assets of the company. A debenture is a bit like a mortgage on a house except that it doesn't just relate to the property but covers all the assets. It's as though the building society could take your knives and forks. There wasn't one so we came up with the idea that we had to create one very quickly.

'Because it was very unusual, although certainly not illegal, we needed someone who had the financial muscle to back us in case the procedure was ever challenged. We thought about Bradford Council.

'The plan was for the Council to loan the football club £100 on the Friday against the security of a debenture. Later that day they would ask City "Please can we have our £100 back?" Bradford City would then say sorry we can't repay because we haven't got any money. That would enable the Council to appoint a receiver.'

The crisis was no major surprise to those in the know. Signs that City were struggling to pay their bills began to emerge towards the end of an eventful 1982–83 season, during which Trevor Cherry succeeded his former England teammate Roy McFarland as player-manager and guided them into a safe mid-table position.

It became clear that Bob Martin's 10-year reign as chairman was coming to an end as rival groups began manoeuvring to take over the club, among them Mike Norman, whose firm Toy City were the shirt sponsors.

City signed 'a world-class centre-back', Roy McFarland, as player-manager. However, Jacko hung on in there and was part of the squad that gained that vital promotion out of the old Fourth Division in 1982.

It was to be the start of the successful modern era of Bradford City, and, when McFarland left and Trevor Cherry and Terry Yorath were put in charge, 'Jacko' was again made captain, and things began to gather pace. From being bottom of the League at one point, 'Jacko' played in eight of the club record of 10 victories on the spin, and attended the special celebration dinner which followed.

Then came the triumph of promotion and the fire. As skipper, 'Jacko' had the job of ensuring all the players were out of the ground and taken safely to a pub overlooking the scene, ironically called the Belle Vue Tavern. He says 'Later, I went straight to the Bradford Royal Infirmary, still in my kit. There were hundreds of people being treated for burns and other injuries. I spent a couple of hours there, trying to comfort and help them. Then I went home to face the media, who were camped on my doorstep.'

His captain's role did not end there, as he and the then-chairman Stafford Heginbotham attended funerals, visited the ill and received cheques for the official fire victims' fund. 'It was a massive job and I made a players' rota for them to do visits and attend fundraising events. I couldn't believe the tremendous spirit of some of the victims. They had 60 percent burns and yet their main concern was for the future of Bradford City. It made you feel very humble, and determined too.'

'Jacko' never did play at Valley Parade again. He played at Odsal Stadium, Leeds Road and Elland Road for City while they were homeless and was then given the golden opportunity to join Newcastle United. It was a shock and a tough baptism as he came up against top-flight strikers, one particular early encounter seeing 'Jacko'

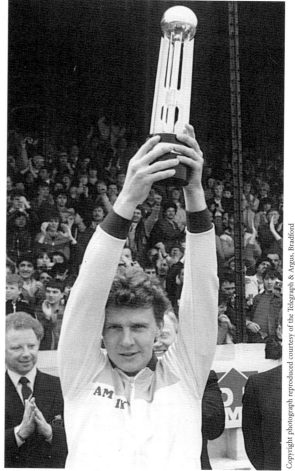

IT'S OURS – Skipper Peter Jackson holds the Third Division Championship trophy in triumph with director Peter Flesher applauding in the background.

battling to tether Irish international striker John Aldridge. He ultimately became Newcastle's Player of the Year, ahead of two also-rans by the name of Beardsley and Gascoigne!

Years on, it was back to Bradford City in the Second Division with Terry Dolan in charge. 'It never worked out for me,' says 'Jacko'. 'My biggest regret is that I came back and let so many down.' When the club were relegated under John Docherty – 'the worst manager ever to run a football club, in my opinion' – 'Jacko' went on a free to Huddersfield and his career took off again for 'four happy years.' He played out his career at

Chester and Halifax and then got the call to manage Huddersfield with Terry Yorath as coach, before being cruelly sacked in favour of Steve Bruce, with whom, ironically, he had started out in his quest for professional soccer as a youngster at Burnley.

Another irony is that 'Jacko' could right now be the manager of Bradford City if he had accepted Geoffrey Richmond's blandishments to give up his job working for a soccer agency.

He reveals 'Sometime after Jim Jeffries's departure in December 2001, I spent four hours on Christmas Eve with Geoffrey Richmond at his home in Leeds. I was flattered to be offered the post and it was all sorted in principle. The money was great and everything was in place. But when I went home that night there was something nagging me. I phoned the chairman on Christmas Day and told him, and he said that if I wasn't 100 percent certain then I shouldn't take it. I didn't and that was that. Today, I have no regrets whatsoever but I still feel flattered to have been asked.'

'Jacko' had no misgivings when he was asked once more to take the reigns at Huddersfield Town, having teamed up with coach Terry Yorath again. When they were unceremoniously booted out of the job the first time around, they had managed to pull off 'The Great Escape', saving Town from almost certain relegation. Rough justice indeed.

In their current second period at Huddersfield, they have achieved promotion from the bottom tier at the Millennium Stadium Play-off Final in 2004, and, last campaign, almost made the First Division play-offs with a superb end-of-season surge. Now they are doing well in a new campaign, with a young but promising squad and high hopes.

1985–86

WITH NO ground of their own after the fire, City led a cruel and difficult nomadic life all season. Chairman Stafford Heginbotham felt it was symbolically and politically important not to leave Bradford even though Leeds United and Huddersfield Town offered their grounds in the short term. It was also more convenient for City's supporters to play in Bradford.

And so it was that Odsal Stadium, the vast and, at that stage, soulless basin used by Bradford Northern Rugby League club, was chosen. The stadium owners, Bradford Council, backed the move and did their level best to help to make it suitable for soccer. By coincidence, £3 million had been spent at Odsal in 1985 in preparation for the World Speedway Championships, but it was such a vast place that many more millions needed to be spent to make it fit for top-class football.

Everyone realised that Stafford was right in principle, but manager Trevor Cherry and his players knew the surface and surrounds were not brilliant for football, to say the least. In any case, Odsal had to be made safe for strict crowd segregation purposes so Leeds and Elland Road were used for 'home' fixtures until it was ready.

The League helped by making City play only four of their first 13 fixtures at 'home', and their first match at Odsal was a League Cup second round, second leg match against Brighton in early October. It was not an auspicious start for, after losing 5–2 at Brighton in the first leg, they were beaten 2–0 at Odsal and so went out of the competition 7–2 on aggregate. However, by the time City got to their Bradford venue for a League match it was the first Saturday in November and winter conditions were setting in: not for nothing did City fans call Odsal 'Ice Station Zebra'. But they won that match, beating Crystal Palace 1–0 thanks to a goal by John Hendrie.

And if conditions were bad for City they were even worse for visiting teams. It was interesting to watch their faces as they arrived at this vast, unfulfilled amphitheatre with an ash road for the team coach to go down into the bowels of the sunken stadium. I remember one visiting journalist who had left the Hawaiian sunshine of Ipswich to arrive at Bradford's answer to Nepal five hours later. He was wearing a light linen jacket, and although I lent him my overcoat he nearly died of hypothermia.

To a great extent the inhospitable stadium worked to City's advantage. They clocked up victories against Palace, Portsmouth, Carlisle and Brighton before Christmas, but in the New Year winter conditions took their toll at the exposed stadium and there were postponements with more matches being switched to Leeds and Huddersfield.

In fact, City didn't play a single match in February, which left them with a large fixture backlog – eight matches in March and eight in April.

In the end, City managed to finish 13th, which was a minor miracle in the circumstances and their 14 'home' wins played a crucial part. They couldn't get back to Valley Parade quick enough, but they would have to wait another half season before they could return to their traditional home.

While everyone's focus was understandably on the fire tragedy and its devastating effect on the whole community of the Bradford district during the summer of 1985, Trevor Cherry had the difficult task of building a team ready for the higher Division – the first time for 48 years that City had played at that level.

With money tight, Cherry made modest additions to his squad, signing goalkeeper Peter Litchfield from Preston, his former Leeds teammate Scottish international winger Arthur Graham from Manchester United and striker Aidey Thorpe from non-League Heanor. However, in December he also signed defender Gavin Oliver from Sheffield Wednesday for £20,000, and he proved to be one of the club's most consistent players in his 10 years at Valley Parade, first at right-back but later in the centre of the defence.

The season also marked the first appearance in City colours of 6ft 4in striker Ian Ormondroyd, known as sticks. He joined them from Bradford non-League club Thackley and he scored three goals in 12 matches towards the end of the season.

City played with a settled side, using only 18 players. Litchfield, Peter Jackson and John

CHAMPIONS – Newly promoted City pose for their pre-season photograph back in traditional claret and amber stripes, proudly parading the Third Division Championship trophy. Note the picture was taken at the Apperley Bridge training ground because Valley Parade was out of use following the fire. Back, left to right: Tony Clegg, Don Goodman, Chris Withe, Dave Evans, Eric McManus, Bobby Campbell, Peter Litchfield, Greg Abbott, Martin Singleton, Bryan Edwards (physiotherapist). Front, left to right: John Hendrie, Stuart McCall, Trevor Cherry (manager), Peter Jackson, Terry Yorath (assistant manager), Mark Ellis, Arthur Graham.

TEMPORARY HOME – View of Odsal Stadium – City's temporary home following the Valley Parade fire – from the huge Rooley Lane terrace.

SILENT MOMENT – Bobby Robson's England team observe the minute's silence at the re-opening of Valley Parade in December 1986. From left: Peter Shilton, Ian Snodin, Steve Hodge, Peter Reid, Derek Mountfield, Alvin Martin, Kevin Keegan, Neil Webb, Cyrille Regis, Tony Cottee.

HAPPY TIMES – Chairman Stafford Heginbotham relaxes with loyal supporter Alan Hannah.

Hendrie were ever presents and Bobby Campbell missed only one match, while Stuart McCall and Greg Abbott missed only four each. Campbell, Hendrie and penalty taker Abbott each scored 10 goals.

1986–87

WHERE TO begin? City were still in inglorious exile at Odsal, Valley Parade was being rebuilt, a prestigious match was being organised for Bradford City's poignant return home… and the council had changed their slogan from 'Mythbreakers' to 'Bradford's Bouncing Back'. Terry Yorath had left to manage Swansea, and Terry Dolan stepped up to Number Two. The team were struggling at the wrong end of the table, but City's half season at Odsal did hold some happy memories, the 2–0 victory over Leeds being one. Unfortunately, some Leeds followers overturned a chip van, spilling boiling fat on to the terraces.

But let's be positive. A revamped stadium was taking shape at Valley Parade, a defiant and symbolic statement that life for Bradford City goes on. The survival instinct is strong. It was to cost £2.6 million, with City finding £650,000, while the disbanding West Yorkshire Metropolitan Council generously gave nearly £1.5 million, with the Football Grounds Improvement Trust stumping up the rest. Safety and comfort were to be the new watchwords, and the architects were the local firm of Waller and Partners.

The crumbling Kop was given properly constructed terracing, modern crush barriers and a roof. It could accommodate 7,000 people. Safe, and safe from the elements, at last. But, of course, the main emphasis was on the main stand. A modern, 5,000-seater now stood on the site of the 1908 relic, which had been the scene of the conflagration that claimed 56 lives. The Bishop of Bradford, Roy Williamson, unveiled a simple bas-relief sculpture commemorating the victims of 11 May 1985. Equally appropriately, Mr Justice Popplewell, who had conducted the public inquiry into the fire, cut the official ribbon for the reopening on 14 December 1986. Bradford City were back to play Bobby Robson's England XI in front of an emotional capacity crowd of 16,000.

The line-up was:

Peter Shilton, Ian Snodin (Trevor Cherry, 80), Steve Hodge, Peter Reid, Derek Mountfield, Alvin Martin (Terry Fenwick, 45), Kevin Keegan, Neil Webb, Cyrille Regis (Frank Worthington, 73), Tony Cottee (Paul Mariner, 55), Franz Carr.

City's team was:

Litchfield, Evans, Cherry (Withe 14), McCall, Jackson (Clegg 45), Oliver, Hendrie, Palin (Yorath 80), Campbell (Leonard 45), Goodman (Ormondroyd 71), Abbott (Ellis 45).

Ref: Neil Midgley (Bolton).

As usual, Stafford Heginbotham pulled off a surprise coup. Everyone knew Kevin Keegan was living in Spain and was 'unable to attend'. Stafford knew differently. He drove over to Manchester Airport where he had arranged for Kevin to arrive and drove him over for the highly-charged and emotional reopening. Typical of both of them; Stafford for making the impossible happen, Keegan for his generosity of spirit and for remembering that he too had started out at a little club not too far down the road.

Naturally, it was tearful. And it takes a lot for my Uncle Ron and my Uncle Jack to cry. I know to outsiders it might sound a bit in the style of 'grim up North', but it was entirely appropriate that our local Hammond Sauce Works Band was chosen for the rendition of the football hymn *Abide With Me*. Who will forget it?

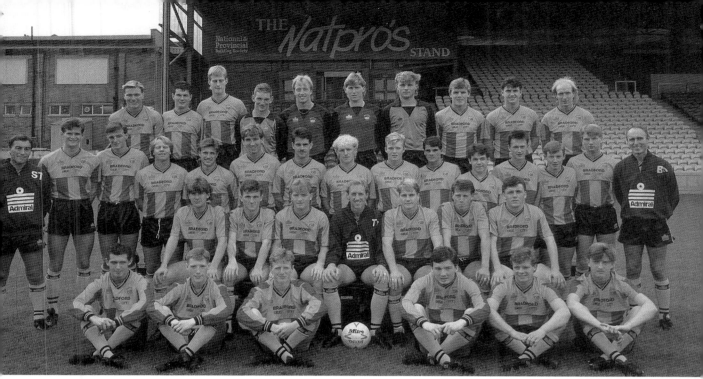

NEAR MISS – The club's playing staff at the start of the 1987–88 season that was to end in a disappointing defeat in the Second Division play-offs. Manager Terry Dolan is seen in the centre with star players Stuart McCall and John Hendrie on either side of him and the apprentices in front. Next to McCall are Karl Goddard and Leigh Palin and on Hendrie's left are Greg Abbott and Robbie Savage. Senior players on the back row include Ian Ormondroyd, Mark Leonard, Gavin Oliver and Ron Futcher along with three senior goalkeepers Paul Tomlinson, Peter Litchfield and Mark Evans. The second row includes Lee Sinnott, Arthur Graham, Brian Mitchell, Dave Evans and Mark Ellis with assistant manger Stan Ternent on the left and physiotherapist Bryan Edwards on the right.

the FA Cup third round and Kennedy scored – a penalty in the 4–2 win over Oxford in the fourth round at the end of January – and made his League debut the following week at home to promotion rivals Millwall.

City ended their eight match run without a win in the League by beating their South East London rivals 1–0 and revived their promotion challenge with a hat-trick of victories, including a 2–1 win against Middlesbrough at Ayresome Park with both goals scored by Ian Ormondroyd.

Starting with the Millwall win, City lost only one of their next 14 matches – a shock and ultimately costly 1–0 home defeat against bottom club Huddersfield Town.

Their consistency in February, March and April left them needing two wins from the last three matches to go up automatically, and after beating Leicester 4–1 at Valley Parade on the next to the last Saturday of the season they were in second place behind leaders Millwall, with a showdown at Aston Villa on May Day Bank Holiday Monday followed by a home match against Ipswich. David Platt did little all game except head home the winner from a free kick, but, to be honest, City under performed on the big occasion in front of a

crowd of 36,423 at Villa Park. So, it was down to Ipswich at home on the last day of the season. Dolan's worst fears were realised. Suspensions caught up, with Hendrie sidelined for the most important game of the season after being harshly sent off at Manchester City two weeks before. It was the only game he missed in four years at the club. If City won, Middlesbrough lost and Villa failed to win, City could still get automatic promotion. City lost 3–2. It was the playoffs against Boro.

The rest we know, as Dolan recalls in his chapter in this book. City won 2–1 at Valley Parade and should have won by four or five. In the second leg in extra time City went down 2–0. Recriminations followed: a row on the coach between Kennedy and Hendrie and a 'difference of opinion' between Dolan and Tordoff.

In the close season McCall went to Everton for £875,000 and Hendrie joined Newcastle for £500,000. They wanted First Division football and Bradford hadn't delivered it. McCall signed for Everton after his 24th birthday, eight years after he had signed as an associate schoolboy with City. He would be back... but, by then, Dolan would be long gone.

STUART McCALL

STUART MCCALL is by common consent Bradford City's most popular player of the modern era.

All supporters have their favourites, but everyone loves Stuart McCall. His relationship with the City faithful goes back more than 20 years and it is easy to see why the flame-haired midfielder has been so popular.

It isn't just that McCall has been at the centre of most of the success City have enjoyed in the last 20 years or so. It's his wholehearted commitment to the game that endears him to the fans, whatever team he plays for.

The term model professional is sometimes over used, but it certainly applies in McCall's case. He always gave his best, no cause was ever lost, no ball was not worth chasing, no opportunity to tackle was missed. His never-waning enthusiasm was an inspiration to everyone.

In an age when players' commitment is sometimes called into question, McCall stood out not only as a shining light of what a footballer should be on the field but also as a wonderful ambassador for the game in the community.

In a career that spanned 24 years, the former Scottish international spent 12 years at Valley Parade, and there are many who regret that he was allowed to leave at the end of the 2002 season as he went on to play an influential part in Sheffield United's successful campaign that saw them reach two Cup semi-finals and the First Division Play-off Final.

How City missed his experience, leadership and commitment as they struggled in the lower half of the table.

McCall was involved in two promotions in his first spell at Valley Parade. Then, after two years at Everton, he moved to Glasgow Rangers and won 40 caps, Scottish League and Cup honours, as well as gaining extensive experience in European football, before returning to lead City to the Premiership.

McCall, who was learning his trade as an apprentice when City won promotion from the Fourth Division in 1982, played a key part in the Third Division Championship season three years later. On his second time with City, he not only helped secure Premiership soccer but also helped keep them in the top flight for two years, against the predictions of all informed opinion.

McCall, now 41, played League football for 24 years, but he vividly remembers how he was 'discovered' by City. He says 'The then-manager George Mulhall and Bryan Edwards came to watch me play for Farsley Celtic Juniors. Only two of us had not been taken on by League clubs. The others had gone to Leeds United, Nottingham Forest or Huddersfield Town. I thought I had missed the boat and would have to go for another occupation.

'I was very small when I signed as a 16-year-old, and I needed building up. Inside six months I had put on a few inches. It helped me to develop quickly, and I enjoyed it, but I was disappointed when George Mulhall left to go back to Bolton. Still, Roy McFarland came in, and I just loved being around the environment of the club. If there was a chance to go on an away trip with the first team, it was a great experience to share in the build up.

'I also used to travel on the supporters' trip to watch the team. I really enjoyed my football. One good thing about being a lower division team was the fact that there were only three apprentices. We trained with the first team from day one. It was a quick learning process and that helped me. The only way I could go was up. You get a better chance with a lower division club and City were in the Fourth Division. It helped me to grow up quickly and keep progressing up the ladder.

STAR MAN – Stuart McCall presented with the match ball by assistant manager Terry Yorath.

Copyright photograph reproduced courtesy of the Telegraph & Argus, Bradford

TOP MEN – Jack Tordoff and Terry Dolan in happy mood.

take your memories away.' Back at Valley Parade, Dolan's journey took him from youth coach to reserve coach to caretaker manager to boss in his own right, under the rule of 'The Unlikely Lads' in the form of chairman Heginbotham and leading director Jack Tordoff.

Dolan says 'They were completely different. Stafford was larger than life, promised everything and was a likeable rogue – good to have around, but you can't have more than one. Jack was completely different, and I respect the fact that Jack had to be different from Stafford. He told you straight and you had to accept it, whereas

Stafford would go about things in a roundabout fashion.'

Which brings us to the major talking point of 1988, and ever since. The issue was whether City should have strengthened the team when they were pushing for promotion to the top flight? Would City have got there if Dolan had been able to secure the two key players he had lined up in principle?

The facts are never simple to get at. Before transfer deadline day in March, City had totted up a 10-match unbeaten run. Naturally, Dolan wanted to strengthen the team for the final push, just as their rivals Villa and Middlesbrough were doing. The latter brought in Reading's prolific striker Trevor Senior, who was to score some very important goals in their remaining matches.

Dolan says he had lined up Andy Townsend for around £300,000 from Southampton, and Reading's Keith Curle – then just breaking through as a potential star – for the same amount. According to Dolan, the board refused to sanction it. He claims that chairman Tordoff told him the team was strong enough. But Ternent, in his book, says he told Tordoff 'Speculate to accumulate. You can always get your money back if necessary by selling McCall and Hendrie.'

When it didn't transpire, Dolan had to go with what he'd got, even though he knew suspensions or injuries could blow the promotion bid off course. City lost to Villa away, David Platt doing little all game except scoring the winner. It was all down to the last match at home to Ipswich.

Dolan's worst fears were realised. John Hendrie was suspended after being sent off at Manchester City. It was a nightmare and so was City's 2–3 defeat by the Tractor Men. Into the play-offs against Middlesbrough. City were 'outstanding' in the first leg at Valley Parade, but only won 2–1, with Senior scoring Boro's vital away goal. The second leg went to extra-time with Boro one up. They scored another, and City's bid for the big time was over.

On the coach home, Hendrie and Mick Kennedy had a spat. Dolan and Tordoff apparently had words. Dolan says 'I never felt as low in my life. The chance to take a team to the top flight had gone.' He tried to put a brave face on it, but the writing was on the wall. McCall was sold to Everton for £875,000; Hendrie went to Newcastle for £500,000 and Ron Futcher went to Port Vale for a knock-down £35,000.

More differences of opinion were to follow. Dolan was given most of the £1.4 million to spend on players but was told by Tordoff not to bring in anyone over the age of 27 'because Jack had the idea that there would be no resale value.' Dolan claims 'That stopped me signing Keith Houchen from Coventry and Terry Connor from Portsmouth. I felt shackled by this policy.'

Ian Banks came in from Huddersfield for £180,000, but it proved impossible for him to live up to the reputation of McCall. Newcastle's Andy Thomas, who cost £80,000, never really clicked, and old favourite Peter Jackson came back for £290,000 from Tyneside, but he too never did himself justice the second time round. Paul Jewell was bought from Wigan for £80,000 and proved to be a useful acquisition.

To make matters worse, Dolan and Ternent fell out with Tordoff over renewed contract talks. As Dolan admits 'One of the problems was that Stan and myself were as stubborn as Jack, and he didn't like it.'

Still, there was excitement for the fans, with a splendid 1–0 FA Cup win over Spurs, Brian Mitchell scoring the all-important solo strike. Then there was the 3–1 League Cup victory over Everton at Valley Parade. However, City lost at home to Bristol City in the next round of the League Cup and were beaten by Hull City 2–1 at Valley Parade in the FA Cup fourth round, with Leigh Palin being sent off. Dolan was called to a board meeting and was sacked there and then. Ternent, who hadn't come in that day, was sacked over the phone.

Dolan admits ' I felt aggrieved, but you have to accept it. I felt as bad that night as I did when we lost the play-offs. I'm Bradford through and through. Looking at my record there I spent two years in charge, spent about £1 million and brought in more than £2 million. Since then, in my other jobs I've spent naff all. If it's not been there, I've never asked for money.'

Final thought? 'Well, deep down, I've always felt the chance to manage Bradford might come again. Fourteen years on, I've done the tough stuff at Rochdale, Hull and York. It's all stood me in good stead.'

JACK TORDOFF

JACK TORDOFF is a highly successful businessman and high up there on the nation's 'rich list', but he still finds time 'to set a few records straight' about the period when he was effectively in charge of the destiny of his beloved Bradford City.

He has taken all the slings and arrows that inevitably fly the way of a Football League club chairman, and knows only too well that football is a robust game with robust people involved, and issues that would test the patience of Job. It is not a world for the faint hearted.

Even so, Tordoff has never felt the need to respond in public to any criticism or claims about decisions he may, or may not, have made... until now.

Now in his 70s, it might be understandable if he took time off from running his Bradford-based JCT 600 motor retail company that he started from scratch as a young man, and that now has a turnover of more than £1 million a day. Not a misprint. That's per day.

But though this former champion rally driver, who was known as 'Gentleman Jack', spends some of his leisure time flying his twin-engined plane round Europe, or on his ocean-going boat at Guernsey, he also keeps his hands firmly on the tiller of his company. He did just that during his tenure of office at Bradford City and got it in the neck from some quarters for keeping a tight rein on the club's purse strings.

However, he rebuffs any suggestion that he was overly tight with the club's, and his own, cash resources when it really mattered. All these years on, he is now willing to set out his side of the story, nowhere more so than on the issue of team strengthening, or lack of it, during the crucial 1987–88 season. That's when City were pipped at the post by Middlesbrough during the final play-offs, failing by a whisker to gain promotion to the coveted top flight of English soccer.

According to the generally-held impression at the time, and claims made since – particularly in books by the then-City assistant manager Stan Ternent and Bradford City hero Stuart McCall – the board seemed reluctant to bring in two players said to have been lined up just before the transfer deadline in March by manager Terry Dolan. In particular, Tordoff was said to have told his management team that the side was strong enough as it was.

Now, years on, Tordoff has broken his silence on the issue to put his side of the story. He claims 'Terry Dolan wanted Keith Curle from Reading, and I told him "Ok, we'll buy him. He's young and quick, and that suits me fine." At the time, Reading were skint and agreed to a £300,000 fee – a record for Bradford – and the player wanted to come. However, the news got out and Wimbledon manager Bobby Gould offered £500,000. I asked Dolan "Do we bid more?" But he told me that it was too much. Those were his exact words,' says Tordoff.

The same claims have been made about the non-signing of another Dolan target, Andy Townsend, then a young squad player with Southampton. Again, according to Tordoff, 'I agreed to bid £250,000 for him. I remember the fee only too well because I was going to pay with my own money. But Bradford City wasn't 'sexy' enough for the player at the time, and he chose Norwich instead. They had Robert Chase at the helm, an attractive ground and facilities and had been in Europe.

'Those are the facts. I would swear that on my children's life. A lot of people seem to have made assumptions that are wrong. These misapprehensions have to be nailed. It's time the truth was known.'

Because City missed out on promotion to the old First Division, influential stars McCall and John

THE 1990s

WHAT a decade this was, reaching its climax in the longed-for return to the top flight of English soccer now called the Premiership, after 77 long years in an often weary wilderness.

It was the Richmond era. Since his no-nonsense entrance, with his 'can do' approach, in January 1994, and his landmark declaration 'I have not come here to preside over mediocrity,' the only way was up.

Who, in all honesty, can say that at the beginning of the 1990s, they could see Bradford City playing in the Premiership by the time of the Millennium? In 1990 the team had by now returned to the third tier of English soccer, the club was deep in debt and the ground still had one side that would not even grace today's Nationwide Conference.

Richmond changed all that. The way he did so was not always pretty. Some would say he was ruthless in the implementation of his plan. He had loaned the club more than £2 million from his personal fortune as part of the unique deal, which saw him 'transferred' as chairman of Scarborough FC to Bradford, with City's chairman David Simpson going the other way. Simpson wanted out of Valley Parade, Richmond wanted a club that could potentially match his ambitions. It was a perfect solution for both parties. The contrast with previous expectations could not be more pronounced, and many of the staff didn't like the changed terms of reference. Many didn't survive the Richmond revolution.

The decade had begun with the often maligned John 'the Doc' Docherty in charge. His long-ball reputation, coupled with his orders from Simpson to clear out costly players bought when they were in a higher division, was not a popular prescription for the Bradford public. He did his job but was sacked in November 1991.

In came Frank Stapleton, the laid-back former Irish international who made a fair stab at his first managerial job as he, and the successful coach Colin Todd, arrested City's decline. Todd went off to Bolton almost as quickly as he came, and with the club hamstrung with a large overdraft, and player-manager Stapleton sidelined after a cartilage operation, thoughts of reaching the play-offs did not materialise.

In came Richmond. Out went eight behind-the-scenes staff, with Stapleton following them four months later. In came Lennie Lawrence, an experienced campaigner with a reputation built at Charlton and Middlesbrough. He knew the score but his more 'seen it all before' style was quite the opposite to that of the perhaps over zealous and certainly 'hands on' approach of Geoffrey Richmond. They lasted 18 months together and both seemed relieved when they parted company.

When Chris Kamara was installed as manager – the first of three insiders to be appointed by Richmond – promotion to Division Two was still the main preoccupation. Amazingly, it was achieved despite the odds being stacked against. In the 1995–96 season, with 16 games left, it seemed unlikely that Bradford would reach the play-offs. City lost just four of those run-in games and claimed bottom spot in the play-offs. They were pitted against Sam Allardyce's higher-placed Blackpool, and made a nightmare start by losing 2–0 at home in the first leg. Kamara changed his tactics for the match at Bloomfield Road, and stunned Blackpool by beating them 3–0. By now the new Midland Road stand was being built. Work started long before the prospect of Wembley glory. Such was Richmond's vision for the club.

Thirty thousand Bradford City fans witnessed their team walk over Notts County 2–0 at Wembley to gain admission back into Division Two. The jigsaw was taking shape.

The next battle was one for survival in the higher Division. Kamara had no real money to spend because most of it was earmarked for the new Midland Road stand. Bosman frees or bargain signings became the norm, with 42 players pulling on the claret and amber shirt that season of 1996–97. With two final wins over Charlton and QPR, City survived and sent Grimsby down.

Sadly for Kamara, he never made it to the end of the 1997–98 season. Big signings had been made by then, but with each one expectancy grew. It had been a major blow when striker 'Flash' Gordon Watson broke his leg just three weeks after signing from Southampton in January 1997. Former Manchester United 'keeper Gary Walsh paid off, but Bolton's John McGinlay hardly fulfilled his goalscoring promise. After he missed a couple of great chances in a third-round tie at Manchester City in

January 1998, and the Bantams were out of the FA Cup, Richmond sacked the manager four days later. Kamara 'had taken the club as far as he could'.

In time-honoured fashion, Kamara's assistant Paul Jewell took over, first as caretaker, then until the end of the season and finally for the next two. It was not a popular choice with everybody, with critics saying it showed a lack of ambition. But Richmond stood by his choice and then made the decision to go for promotion to the Premiership, with money being made available to strengthen the squad.

The rest, as they say, is history. Fans' favourite Stuart McCall returned to Valley Parade, striker Lee Mills was bought for £1 million, Gareth Whalley and Ashley Westwood were signed from Crewe and Steven Wright came down from Glasgow Rangers.

With five months still to go to the millennium, City kicked off in the Premiership. Team strengthening brought in David Wetherall, Gunnar Halle, Lee Sharpe, Dean Saunders and Matt Clarke. The team was dubbed 'Dad's Army', but they did the job and, against all predictions, survived for another season. It was a truly exciting year for the fans, especially the last gasp, last game victory over Liverpool, which secured survival. Ironically, if the club had been relegated, the financial disaster of two years on would probably not have occurred. Parachute payments would have tided the club over. Unfortunately, Richmond's self-admitted 'six weeks of madness' was about to unfold. It would end in tears. Poor old John Docherty. His managerial 'marriage' to Bradford City was never made in Heaven.

1990–91

'THE DOC', an inevitable nickname from the start, came in with a little over a month of the 1989–90 season to go, and City were on a downward spiral towards relegation just five years after they had broken the stranglehold of 48 years in the lower divisions The team's morale was down and the crowd was not far behind them.

After coming to terms with the drop, 'the Doc's' remit was clear – get rid of the expensive players and those who had failed to click at Valley Parade. Out went Ian McCall, moving back north to Dunfermline for £100,000; Neil Woods went to Grimsby in the August for £82,000; Dave Evans returned to Halifax Town on a free transfer and Alan Davies went back to Swansea in part exchange for Robbie James.

A month into the new season, Peter Jackson went on a free transfer to Huddersfield Town just two years after City spent £290,000 to bring him back from Newcastle. It was a new lease of life for 'Jacko' who had an excellent four-year stint at Leeds Road before moving to Chester and then Halifax to end his playing career. Finally, in January 1991, 'the Doc' moved on Tony Adcock, returning to his former club Northampton.

Docherty's big signing in the 1990 close season was Sean McCarthy, who cost £250,000 from Plymouth, and the bustling striker proved to be a prolific scorer in more than three years at Valley Parade.

His other signings were from his old club Millwall with 19-year-old defender Phil Babb and striker Stephen Torpey the best – other Millwall boys who arrived at Valley Parade were midfield players Darren Tracey, Darren Morgan and Wes Reid and left-back Alan Dowson.

When Babb was given a 'free' at The Den, he phoned Docherty for advice. He said simply 'Get on the next train to Bradford.' Babb did just that and restored his career at Valley Parade before being sold to Coventry for £300,000. He joined Liverpool in a £2 million-plus deal and later

WELSH WIZARD – Robbie James – the former Welsh international moved back to Wales after a two-year spell at Valley Parade to become player-coach at Merthyr Tydfil, but tragically died while playing them aged a mere 42.

moved to Sporting Lisbon before ending his career at Sunderland. Torpey was never a fans' favourite, but was a strong, bustling centre-forward. He joined Swansea at the end of his three-year contract and helped Scunthorpe to gain promotion in the 2004–05 season.

City, who started badly, recovered in the second half of the season to finish eighth after winning their last two matches – away to Swansea and

Parade. Not a trick was missed by the astute Richmond. Now the big question was could Kamara keep City up?

1996–97

NEVER MIND the start of the season, what a fantastic finish! The battle to stay in the Second Division went right down to the wire. It was a chairman's dream. Crowds picked up enormously for the nail-biting finish.

Nine days and three matches to go, the first one was away at Danny Wilson's Barnsley, who were League leaders and going for that all-important jump to the Premiership. It was no disgrace for Bradford to lose 2–0 in the circumstances, but it took an extra sliver off the nails.

General Election night that May will long be remembered for the phrase 'And I declare the winner to be... Bradford City.' At another count Tony Blair did quite well too. At Valley Parade it was tight but there was no re-count. City beat Charlton 1–0. The claret and amber rosette was worn with pride. Now, it was all down to the last matches. Bradford v QPR at home and Grimsby v Southend. The Wool Men or the Fish Men, which would it be for the chop?

No problem. City crushed QPR 3–0. Grimsby beat Southend by the even bigger margin of 4–0 but still went down. Kamara had done his job and kept City up. The axe would not fall yet.

In fact, he had done a simply marvellous job. Richmond had told him that because the new Midland Road stand was taking the cash he had to make do and mend. He used his imagination and

WADDLE SIGNS – Manager Chris Kamara introduces former England international Chris Waddle.

PLAY-OFF HEROES – *Mark Stallard, scorer of the second goal at Wembley, in action at the Play-off Final.*

Des Hamilton puts City in front.

NEW BOYS – The 1995 close season signings, (from left) Ian Ormondroyd, Gavin Ward, Jon Ford, Nicky Mohan, Andy Kiwomya, Tommy Wright and Chris Dalby.

the soccer agents who specialised in bringing over exotic-sounding but cheap overseas players. It was high risk, but it was good business. Lots of players. Lots of changes. Lots of interest. Decent crowds. Lots of revenue. Simple equation really.

No less than 42 players were used that season. A Brazilian here. A Costa Rican trialist there. A Portuguese find unveiled. A Swede, a Swiss... the list went on and on. Nearly every week the *Bradford Telegraph & Argus* and the *Yorkshire Post* had a new offering to write about. It was certainly exotic, novel and very interesting. Bargain buys and Bosman frees included Marco Sas, Erik Regtop, Edinho, Sergio Pinto, Robert Steiner, Ole Bjorn Sundgot and Magnus Pehrsson, known by one soccer-writing wag as 'Missing Person'. The language problems alone were immense. David Markham was despatched to interview Sergio Pinto at the farmhouse where he was billeted at

Esholt, next to Bradford's sewage works. 'There we were, the farmer, his wife, Pinto and me at the kitchen table, with pungent farm and sewage smells wafting by. He spoke no English, I spoke no Portuguese. What he made of it, who knows!'

But despite the 'International Brigade' policy, Kamara's ace 'find' was an Englishman through and through. His signing of former England maestro Chris Waddle was an act of sheer genius. He delighted the crowds with his silky skills and gave the players a massive morale boost as well as handy hints on how to improve their game. It was like having an extra coach on board, as well as a scintillating ball player on the pitch. Who will ever forget his wonder goal in Bradford's shock 3–2 fourth round FA Cup victory at Everton? It was vintage Waddle. Two months later Waddle was on his way to Sunderland, but what a six months of entertainment City fans had.

controversially, a penalty was awarded. Peter Beagrie duly obliged. Five minutes into the second half Beagrie doubled City's advantage. Then Dean Windass sent Valley Parade into party mood with a late strike to make it 3–0. More importantly, it put City one point above the Dons.

The twists and turns went on. City lost at Leicester and the Dons grabbed a point to level peg with City on 33 points. It was all down to the last games, and the Dons had the advantage. If they won at the Dell they stayed up on goal difference. City had to win their last home match and it was against Gerard Houllier's Liverpool, who needed to win to qualify for the Champions League. All the odds favoured Wimbledon to stay up.

It's a match no one will ever forget. The 13th minute in particular. City won a free-kick, Gunnar Halle sent over the cross and the unmarked David Wetherall planted his header into a corner of the net. Richmond was pumping the air with glee, just as he did when Wayne Bridge scored for Southampton against Wimbledon 57 minutes into the Dell Boys' game. Then, Marian Pahars doubled the Saints' lead to send a crowd 260 miles away into paroxysms of delight.

City were safe and deserved to be. They had warranted another crack in the Premiership. It went to everyone's head, including that of Geoffrey Richmond. But by the time of his 'six weeks of madness' that summer, Paul Jewell had quit. What else could happen?

2000–01

IT STARTED out in a jet used by the Aga Khan. It ended in a crash landing. From Bradford in Europe to Bradford in tatters. Who could have foreseen what was to happen as a consequence of City's second year in the Premiership?

At first, it was another great adventure and the fans loved it. So did the chairman, as the great adventure began with City in Europe. Not exactly the Champions League, but the match against Lithuania's FK Atlantas in the Inter-Toto Cup was

a start, and it was a potential route to the UEFA Cup proper.

A small group of people stood in the foyer at the Bradford-Leeds Airport waiting for a plane, which had broken down at Stansted. The team were despatched in a smaller replacement plane to the far-away Baltic state, but some officials, half a dozen reporters and a group of avid fans were left behind. Free drinks and food was arranged by chairman Geoffrey Richmond, who had ordered another plane to be sent for.

Hours later, it arrived. The last word in luxury. It was an executive jet often used by the Aga Khan. Supporters and media men sat in luxury armchairs, with waitress service at proper tables with tablecloths and full silver service. It appeared that Richmond had even ordered a tailwind to help the plane along its urgent journey. Arrangements had been made too for the special flight to land at a military airport near the ground, a coach taking the party straight off to their hotel. No matter that the home ground of Atlantas resembled a building site. Many of the stand seats had been stolen, the floodlights were a bit dicky and the field of action looked more like a field that had been ploughed. Mere detail. Premiership side Bradford City won 3–1.

Off the field, the main attraction was the 'Club Paradox.' Maybe, with self-contradiction, it was meant to be 'Paradise'. In actual fact, 'Club Bizarre' might have been more apt as the star cabaret act came on – a rotund, red-bearded Lithuanian wearing a kilt and singing *Auld Lang Syne!* After it was all over, Richmond and his retinue returned on the Aga Khan plane. The Press were now back on the milk flight.

The return pre-season leg at Valley Parade was also quite a novel experience. With work under way to transform the main stand into a two-tier grand stand worthy of a Premiership side, there was no cover. The heavens opened, everyone got soaked, despite the club's thoughtfulness in issuing plastic smocks to spectators. City won 4–1 and were through to the next round, and the handful of Lithuanian supporters who had travelled to

RECORD SIGNING – David Hopkin who joined City from Leeds United for £2.5 million.

Bradford disappeared into the ether as illegal immigrants and were never seen again. Such was Bradford City's entry into Europe. Remarkable, by any standards.

Incidentally, City had a new manager by now. Paul Jewell had walked out on the club on Monday 19 June 2000, barely a fortnight before City's Inter-Toto Cup campaign, which he had so bitterly opposed. Two days later, he was unveiled as manager at First Division Sheffield Wednesday.

Jewell's unassuming assistant Chris Hutchings, a one-time Chelsea reserve player and a thoroughly decent guy into the bargain, had been looking after the shop. But who would be called on to the flight deck on a permanent basis? Richmond was, of course, already in the cockpit, and it was no major surprise when he announced grandiloquently 'We are leaning towards an internal appointment.'

Only Stuart McCall and Hutchings could be in the frame, and to outside observers McCall's power base and popularity might prove a stumbling block. The names of experienced managers were, of course, put forward – Danny Wilson, Bruce Rioch and Joe Kinnear among them. But Richmond preferred his own internal successor, adding 'There are many advantages of an internal appointment. The greatest asset we have is the tremendous team spirit in the dressing room, and both Stuart and Chris have played their part in that.'

It was no surprise when Hutchings was announced as Jewell's successor. Even he had to smile when the national Press reacted with a 'Who's he?' response. The fans' reaction was mixed. Some saw the logic of doing it 'the Liverpool way'. Others were sceptical of Richmond's motives, though he had delivered so far so why not again?

Big things were about to happen in the shape of those shock summer signings. They left the fans excited and exhilarated, but were described later by Richmond himself as being made during 'six weeks of madness'. Not many called them mad at the time.

Letters of contract were signed with each fresh day. The postman certainly knocked more than once. New players came in with every delivery. Peter Atherton and Ian Nolan arrived free of charge, but on Premiership wages, from demoted Sheffield Wednesday. Then came Leeds United's David Hopkin for a cool £2.5 million, still a club record. It would cost City dearly when they paid him out to end his contract. Dan Petrescu arrived on a four-year contract, costing £1 million from Chelsea, to last just six months before he was paid to leave in January. Three quarters of his signing fee was said to have been paid to move him off the pay roll. Ashley Ward came in for £1.5 million on a four-year contract and a reputed £18,000 a week.

But the show-stopper of them all was Benito Carbone, the jewel in Richmond's crown. The chairman took his new manager off to Italy to sign the one-time Sheffield Wednesday and Villa man on a four-year contract and on a 'free'. The ultimate snag was that he was on that four-year contract and on a staggering £40,000 per week. The club also put him up in a house worth £750,000 in the high-roller belt of north Leeds.

Now, no one doubted the stunning talents of Carbone when he was on song and fully engaged, but it was a bit much to expect the Press to forget his much-publicised tantrums, his rows and his past record at both Wednesday and Villa. He had not been popular in the Hillsborough dressing room for a start, and once when he reported for duty he found a baby's outfit hung on his changing room peg. He had a history of taking his bat and ball home. But the Bradford fans didn't want to know. Any such questions at the public Press conference to unveil him were greeted with a ferocious reaction. 'Negative, that's what you are,' bellowed many of the 500 excited fans whom Richmond had invited for his big moment in history. 'Give Benny a chance. You've got it in for us just because we're not fashionable like Man United or Leeds.' That, understandably, but sometimes hysterically, was the reaction to any critical or questioning faculty, and Richmond

On the way, he had helped deliver the dream of a Wembley promotion in 1996. He had previously delivered a new Midland Road stand well before attendances required it. But it was there when City went up into the Second Division via that Wembley Play-off Final, and it symbolically rubbed out the near-50 year long embarrassment of having one side of the ground resemble that of Farsley Celtic. The stand was part of the jigsaw that Richmond – the architect of progress, the man of vision, the Grand Vizier – was putting together. Would the stand cost the club dear? 'It will pay for itself in five years, and if it's too small then we'll pull it down and build another,' said Richmond expansively.

His vision was permanent Premiership status and a ground to match. He had the vision to make it happen... but it all ended in tears and financial disaster. As with many Grand Viziers before, he had built an empire. But the club then over-reached itself and when the pack of cards crumbled, for once it got out of Richmond's control.

To the fan and the outside observer, the near-nine years of Richmond's rein were fascinating, riveting, exhilarating and exciting times. Many observers still claim that he achieved more in nine years than had been achieved in the previous 90. Yet it ended in tears. Was it worth it? Two years of the heady heights for a legacy of financial doom and gloom. Clearly, Richmond's vision was, in retrospect, over ambitious and the club nearly paid the highest price of all. It so nearly went out of existence. Only a £2.6 million deal with the Professional Footballer's Association and the huge rescue investment of the Rhodes and Gibb family saved the club.

But the football fan is used to crises, drama and the machinations of high finance. The game today seems to exist in a Disney fairy world to most ordinary folk. Every day there's a new club facing the prospect of going bust. At one time there was a Leicester here (£50 million debt at that point), a Derby there (£20 million), then Leeds United (reputedly £100 million at its height), then throw in Bradford City (£36 million). There have been plenty more in trouble since.

So do the fans 'forgive' Richmond for his apparent financial folly, that included his 'six weeks of madness' in the splash-out on the likes of Benito Carbone, Dan Petrescu, David Hopkin, Peter Atherton, Ian Nolan and later Stan Collymore. That big question remains: Was it worth it? Well, that is up to every individual to answer for themselves. We each have our view, and opinion is still divided.

But who was this man at the centre of all this drama and controversy? Why and how did this outsider end up at Bradford City? He was not from the city itself. He had never supported them in his life.

Fans and the press often saw only the veneer of charm and consideration. Richmond never forgot the salesman's manner, born out of his early years slogging the streets as a salesman of the old Arthur Mee Encyclopaedia. But managers saw his ruthless side, his wish to control the club's destiny and those around him. He was relentless in his ambition for the club and for himself. The oxygen of publicity and the high-octane fuel of public acclaim seemed to drive him on. If you were with him, fine. If you were against him, you were finished.

His philosophy is undoubtedly of the 'You can't make an omelette without breaking eggs' variety. His single-minded and self-admitted will to succeed was shown clearly in the world of business. He made his millions out of car stickers, then took over the ailing Ronson cigarette lighter company in Leeds and turned it into a financial success. He said he wanted to be a millionaire by the time he was 39. He made it, with several spare millions and years to spare.

He was offered a stake in little Scarborough Football Club and became the leading light there, bringing in sponsorship from the McCain frozen food company.

Scarborough wasn't big enough for his ambitions. 'Not enough hinterland... not enough chimney pots,' he said later. He wanted somewhere bigger with more potential. Eighty miles away in Bradford, the Valley Parade club had a large overdraft and the board were looking for an 'out.' Quite simply, Richmond did a swap. chairman David Simpson became chairman of Scarborough, and Richmond took over at Bradford.

His impact was dramatic. If he was prepared to loan the club more than £2 million to bale them out he wanted a return on his investment. The club had to be made lean and fit. What better way was there to make this happen than being in there every working hour of the day, controlling events, cutting out inefficiency and exploiting every commercial opportunity. Pro-active, hands-on control. That was the Richmond way and, of course, managers and staff didn't always like it.

He clearly didn't take to the idea of existing manager Frank Stapleton staying on, or others on the payroll. Out went the physio, the chief scout, the chief executive and others behind the scenes. And out went Stapleton four months later. Richmond had arrived.

The Inside Story

GEOFFREY RICHMOND got used to being criticised for being too hands-on and for 'wanting to be the manager, as well as chairman.'

Of course, cricket-loving Richmond would play the straight bat to such charges, insisting that he was, of course, simply the chairman.

But with almost theatrical relish, chairman Richmond would smile impishly, and, in playful mood, retort that if he WAS the manager, then he hadn't done a bad job, eh?

To most fans, that was the reality. As one former Tory Prime Minister used to say 'You've never had it so good.' For those who remembered the frustrating and largely unsuccessful days of the old Third and Fourth Division, that was certainly true enough, as City rose meteorically to the dizzy heights of the Premiership.

Richmond had another ace up his sleeve too. He was determined that Bradford City would have a ground to match his high ambitions for the team. He laid out the blueprint, then purposefully bulldozed his plans through. He even got the

Queen to open the new Midland Road stand. It left fans dazzled by the speed and scale of it all. Truly, they'd never had it so good!

It can't have been easy for those working under him. But to paraphrase the thoughts of chairman Richmond, when does the easy life produce results? Certainly those managers who served under him are now emboldened enough to tell it how it was, even though many of them initially agreed to so-called 'gagging' clauses in return for decent pay-offs when they left.

But if Richmond feels free to talk about them, then in the tough, knock-about world of professional soccer he cannot complain if they finally feel free to tell their own stories and give their own views. The chapters on Frank Stapleton, Lennie Lawrence, Chris Kamara, Paul Jewell, Terry Yorath and Jim Jeffries in particular make for interesting and illuminating reading. Of course, having moved on to pastures new, Richmond takes it on the chin, in time-honoured soccer fashion, though to balance matters he does have his say on the issues and the personalities, giving his own fascinating, no-punches-pulled take on it all.

So how hard was it working for a highly-ambitious boss who was in the office virtually every working day before 8am – first to arrive, last to leave; who had a 'can do' and a 'will do' approach to life; who had a deep resentment of failure and an equally deep will to succeed.

Did he pull all the strings behind the scenes? Did he choose managers from within the club's ranks to keep them grateful and under his thumb? Was it healthy for a football club to be run along such lines? What were his motives? Personal glory? Financial dividends? The limelight? Fulfilment of a dream?

Questions, questions! Perhaps an equally pertinent question was did the fans care who was really in charge as long as the club continued to advance in meteoric fashion, while Valley Parade was being turned into a ground to be proud of?

One man who saw it all from the inside and alongside Richmond was Shaun Harvey, right-

PREMIERSHIP SALVATION – David Wetherall heads the crucial goal that enabled City to beat Liverpool 1–0 in the last match of the 1999–2000 season, securing their stay in the Premiership.

hand man to the chairman in his days at Scarborough FC and then at Bradford for the near nine-year Richmond era. Harvey has now moved on to become chief executive at Leeds United, but his observations give an insight into the way Richmond worked and the way he made things happen.

On the 'Who really governs' front, Harvey recalls 'I remember a famous interview with Geoffrey Richmond when he was accused of wanting to be the club manager and of picking the side. That was when he retorted that he was chairman of the club, but if he was the manager he hadn't done a bad job.

'He was certainly "hands on," much to the intense irritation of some people. However, people at the club had never been as well paid or rewarded for their hard work and dedication, which is a point that people often forget.'

Harvey is also adamant 'The success of Bradford City in those times was directly the result of Geoffrey Richmond's "hands on" approach, though the route of getting there was often unconventional. The skill is being able to separate the good things from the bad, preferably without the benefit of hindsight. In my opinion, life at Bradford City with Geoffrey Richmond had been a massive success for staff and supporters alike up until the summer of 2000.'

Harvey also gives an insight into the 'six weeks of madness' in the summer of 2000, when the club signed high-roller players on long contracts, the most controversial being the deal with the highly skilful but previously temperamental Italian ace Benito Carbone.

Harvey was with Richmond and manager Chris Hutchings that August night in Milan when Carbone was induced to sign. He says 'The decision to give him a four-year contract at £40,000-a-week has been severely criticised since. However, the theory was that there would be no shortage of clubs prepared to take him off our hands, possibly even with a transfer fee, if we were relegated.

'During the long negotiations, there were many twists and turns. However, once Richmond had agreed to go to £40,000 a week, Carbone was still undecided.

At that point an Italian agent said he believed Teddy Sheringham would sign from Manchester United for that sort of money. He rang Alex Ferguson's mobile immediately and left a message for him to come back to us. But before he got a response, which was not surprising since it was now the early hours of the morning, Carbone came back and said he would sign. Who knows what would have happened had we got back to England without him, although I'm sure Teddy Sheringham does not know about our interest to this day!'

Harvey adds 'Having preserved our status in the Premier League, the self-confessed "six weeks of madness" was the downfall of the club in terms of relegation and then administration. However, it is fair to say that hindsight plays a major part in this view. I remember the match against Chelsea at the start of that season when we won 2–0, beating one of the most talented sides in the Premiership out of sight, with Benito Carbone being very influential.

At the end of that game, the talk on the terraces was whether we would qualify for Europe not whether we would survive! I wouldn't go as far as that, but having witnessed that performance I found it very difficult to think that the signings, including Carbone, were foolhardy.'

So what of Richmond's grandiose plans to build a stadium fit to grace the Premiership? Was that foolhardy? It was Richmond's grand plan ultimately to have a 35,000-seater stadium that would be adequate for the club's new requirements and give the club the status that went with it. But was the commitment to a £7.4 million new two-tier main stand a leap too far?

Harvey admits 'By the second year in the Premiership contractors had already begun work on the new stand, shop and office complex, and I became worried about it, but the work could not be stopped.' He adds, somewhat controversially, 'Of all the financial decisions that were made at that time, the one to build the stand was the one that no one would have argued with because it was a major step forward in the club's potential to compete in the Premiership. While it came to represent the club's single biggest debt, the club now at least has the capacity to return at some stage to the top flight.'

'However, since we knew relegation to the First Division would be a hammer blow – and effectively from Christmas we knew our fate – our number one aim was to shed as many of the players as we could to bring in as much cash as possible. The first year back in the First Division was always going to be a struggle, both financially and on the field of play. So it proved, and on 16 May 2002 the club went into administration – the genuine low point.'

With Richmond gone and the new Rhodes-Gibb partnership in power trying to save and then sort out the club, Harvey provided continuity and experience. Having been at Valley Parade for nine years, he knew the inside track and was seen as a vital 'player' in helping to sort out the club's future.

Harvey stayed on throughout the first administration, but moved on to his lucrative job at Leeds United, where he rejoined the Richmond family who were bidding to become a part of the new regime at the time. Harvey had come a long way from his early days as club secretary at Scarborough FC, but he reveals that even before he began his new job he discovered that Richmond had put Scarborough on the market, a move which caused shock waves for those who worked there. Typically, Richmond told Harvey not to worry. It would be all right – and it was!

Then came the amazing 'double transfer', which took the ambitious Richmond to Bradford

City and the then-Valley Parade chairman David Simpson to Scarborough. No one but Richmond could have thought up such a ground-breaking 'swap' deal.

Harvey followed suit and reveals 'In typical Richmond fashion, he said there was a lot of work to be done and changes to be made at Bradford. He first dismantled the loss-making lottery and then sorted out the staff. He sent out the message that the stadium he inherited wasn't big enough or good enough for his aspirations for the club. First the Midland Road Stand was built, and over the subsequent years the ground was transformed.'

Harvey sees the Wembley play-off victory against Notts County in 1996, with 30,000 City fans there, as being positive proof that Richmond's vision for the club was taking shape. City got to Wembley by beating Blackpool in the two-leg semi-final, and perhaps Harvey was getting the hang of Richmond's forte for the caustic sound bite when he said afterwards 'This victory is for the 3,700 supporters who turned up and watched us play Notts County in the League two months ago.'

When Chris Kamara's reign came to an end, Richmond himself came up with the back-handed compliment 'He has taken the club as far as he could.' As Harvey says 'It's a phrase that has been adopted elsewhere since, but it was used first at Valley Parade.'

'Richmondisms' were certainly to be savoured. His measured and ever so sincere responses often reminded you of the style of Margaret Thatcher. There was a certain finality about his utterances, as if to tell you 'That is the end of the conversation.' Once, when asked if the club was having a cash-flow problem, he told the inquirer in an almost condescending manner 'No, no, no, no! (pause) Just a spot of financial indigestion.' Sadly, in the end, the dyspepsia was unable to be treated by a couple of Rennies.

When he rang the local paper to reveal that he had dispensed with the services of the club's chief executive, he said 'For some time there have been two chief executives at this club – one, I might add, who is unpaid.' When asked when the other one would be leaving, Richmond answered in a hushed tone 'Today, (pause) with immediate effect.' End of conversation.

His relationship with the Press was fine, providing you didn't cross him. He loved being on TV, on the radio or in the papers. Once riled, he would refuse to talk to certain reporters who had dared to criticise his actions or who had alternative sources of information. But knowing the usefulness of the media, he usually made his peace, in his own good time.

The exception was the Press Conference to unveil the signing of Benito Carbone, held in front of 500 excited Bradford City fans. Legitimate questions about his temperament and his loyalty record at other clubs were laughed out of court, much to the fury of the national Press who attended, and Richmond treated several of them with apparent derision. Was he beginning to think he didn't need the Press? That he was walking on water? Nowadays, he regrets his treatment of them, but adds impishly 'Sky told me it made for wonderful live TV.'

National radio had been a platform too. During the immediate post-Kamara days, Richmond was genuinely outraged by David Mellor's comments on Five Live's network sports phone-in 606, speculating that colour might have played a part in Kamara's sacking. Richmond demanded airtime and got his pound of flesh in a bruising encounter with Mellor. The Richmond era was never boring.

Controversy was never far away. Once City were relegated from the Premiership, Richmond was one of the main supporters of a breakaway Phoenix League of top First Division clubs, hopefully to be joined by Rangers and Celtic. With fears that the Premiership and its linked Phoenix League would be exclusive and sealed from the rest, the remaining Nationwide clubs were far from happy.

So how will Richmond be judged as fans look back over City's 100-year history? It's obvious that he was not easy to work for judging by the strength of feeling expressed by virtually every former manager. Yet, no one complained about the high salaries and the seemingly-constant advance of the club's fortunes. He had taken the club into the Premiership and into Europe, albeit via the back door. The Inter-Toto Cup competition may not have been the Champions League, but the steak dinners in Lithuania, Holland and Russia still tasted good.

Many observers and fans ask the question 'What did Richmond get out of it, apart from the glory?' Financially, he did very well, and, certainly, he loved the limelight and the trappings of soccer success. He cut quite a commanding figure, arriving at the ground in a top-of-the-range convertible Bentley, which was leased for him by the club, an extravagance that may well astound loyal Bradford City fans

The post-Richmond regime claim it was quite an eye-opener when they discovered the extent of the club's financial problems. Most of the fabric of the ground was leased too, rather than owned outright by the club.

It has been said that City experienced more in the nine years with Richmond at the helm than they had in the previous 90.

It may have been a roller coaster ride, but as local reporter Simon Parker said at the time 'Without Richmond, the City faithful would never have taken in the view – however fleeting – from the very top.'

In the end, the accumulated £36 million 'debt' brought in the administrators and it all ended in tears. Richmond is on record as saying 'It has created unbelievable heartache and worry for everyone connected with the club.' But he added 'Some of the days we've had here over the last few years have been completely and totally unforgettable. Supporters will take those with them until their dying day – and they can happen again.'

Whether or not that is a realistic aspiration, no one would argue with the sentiments expressed.

The Summer of Madness

IN THE summer of 2000 Geoffrey Richmond and his Bradford City entourage chinked their wine glasses together in a fashionable Milan restaurant as they toasted the impending signing of Italian superstar Benito Carbone.

Two years on, Richmond rued the day he had signed the former Sheffield Wednesday striker on £40,000 a week, with accommodation in a £750,000 club-owned house in the smart end of north Leeds. The inability to ship out the man who had become a Milanese millstone – by now a highly expensive luxury for second-flight Bradford City – would be a major contribution to City's slide into deep financial trouble.

Eventually, it is reported that the club had to pay about £750,000 just to get rid of Carbone in a bid to reduce the reputed £36 million of debts that City would be liable for if the club went into liquidation. Years on, through gritted teeth, the chain smoking Richmond pulls no punches when he says 'He described me as "the worst chairman in football." Well, as far as I'm concerned, the little boy should grow up. He will realise in time that we helped make a talented but under-achieving player into a multi-millionaire, a player who, in my opinion, gave back far less than we gave to him.

'We looked after him as though he was a member of the Royal Family. Yet, in the end, he resisted all efforts to help the club he claimed to love. I personally think he was too comfortable, being paid handsomely and living in a lovely house. Even when we put him on loan to Middlesborough, who wanted to buy him, I was told his demands, and the way he expressed his demands, were too high and unacceptable. In my opinion, he was greedy.'

Richmond blames Carbone for being 'one of the two hammer blows' that hit the club and forced it into administration. Years later, as the former Valley Parade chairman draws on his umpteenth cigarette, he recalls 'There were two hammer blows within days – the ITV digital demise that blew a hole of £4 million in our balance sheet, and the collapse of the Carbone move to Boro, which I reckon cost us £5 million over two years. We were forced to bring in professional financial advisors and they told us that we would be at great personal risk if we continued trading whilst insolvent.

'A cash injection of between £6 and 7 million was needed immediately.

'Without it, we had no choice but to go into administration during the May of 2002.'

The rest of the dismal story is known to every Bradford City fan, as the club – just a year short of its Centenary – so nearly folded completely. And that is no exaggeration.

So where did it all go wrong? Both Richmond and the Rhodes family agree wholeheartedly that a prime cause was what the former chairman admitted later to be his 'six weeks of summer madness' after the club had survived in the Premiership.

Put simply, chairman Richmond believed he could secure City's continued future as a top-flight club by bringing in a pantheon of star signings.

Carbone was the biggest luminary, followed ultimately by the often wayward Stan Collymore. Exiting for the fans, but neither was in the Bradford City mould.

Richmond had secured finance house loan funding of £11 million for players, who they valued with an ambitious saleable value of £32 million, a figure that the chairman thought was well over the top. But he says 'Even so, if we had stayed in the Premiership there would have been no problem in meeting our commitments. Only if we were relegated would there be a potential problem.

'But even then, I thought we would be able to sell off players for cash and release others on 'frees' to reduce the wage bill. I wasn't then aware of the impending ITV digital deal collapsing, nor the subsequent Carbone scenario.'

The recruiting started with the signing of Peter Atherton and Ian Nolan, experienced Premiership campaigners who came 'free' but on high wages from Sheffield Wednesday. Then City beat off competition for Leeds United midfield player David Hopkin from Manchester City, who had bid £3 million according to Richmond. Bradford City landed him for £2.5 million, but after an injury-hit record of playing only nine games, the club paid him £750,000 to go – back to Crystal Palace – with Richmond admitting 'I wish in retrospect he had gone over the Pennines.'

City had no more luck with the near £1 million signing of Dan Petrescu from Chelsea, paying another £700,000 to move him on – to South-ampton – after a combination of disappointing form and looming financial problems made it necessary to remove him off the wage bill. It was the economics of the mad house, though the wages bill was being slashed when it became obvious that City would not survive in the top flight.

Carbone was the icing on the administrator's cake, so to speak. The club were confident of shifting him to Italy, but there were no takers for the man who had something of a reputation for being a temperamental star, even though he hardly ever proved a difficulty at Valley Parade, with his meticulous and thorough training regime. Richmond banked on Middlesborough taking him after his initial loan period, but he claims 'Their officials told me that they couldn't live with his demands, and the way he expressed them.'

City's wage bill, topping £14 million a year at its peak, was certainly crippling the by now desperate club, which also had huge loan repayments for both the new main stand – £7.5 million – and the loans taken out for both the tilt at promotion and then for the second Premiership season, not to mention the lease repayments on just about every fixture and fitting at the ground.

Richmond says the difference between assets and liabilities was about £11 million, and says he is 'hurt' by the so-called debt figure of £36 million that was banded around. That figure was only if the club went into liquidation.

'It was a mechanism to keep the creditors from pulling the plug. It kept them in administration,' he claims. He says the £36 million figure was based on the assumption that the club would not play a match the next season, that every single player was paid up for the rest of his contract, that no Premiership parachute money would be paid, that the ground had no value whatsoever and that the players had no transfer value. In other words, the worst possible scenario, if everything did go pear-shaped.

To keep the club going during administration, the Rhodes family started to put their own hard cash into the club, rather than the previously secured guarantees against money borrowed. Richmond himself had put no money into the club, other than the initial unsecured loan of £2.3 million when he originally took over, a sum which was paid back with interest. Both families had received millions out of the controversial dividend payments in the first Premiership season. But as the Rhodes family dipped into their pockets, they asked Richmond to do likewise, only to get the reply 'I am not in a position to help the club financially.'

On the dividend and payment front, Richmond admits the figures freely, accepting fully that the Rhodes family paid him an initial £3 million for their 49 percent of shares to buy into the club. In the Premiership season, the Richmonds and associated companies took a £4 million dividend, and Chairman Richmond admits he was twice paid a £250,000 'consultancy fee', the first being part of the dividend payment, the second being a stand-alone fee. On top of this, he freely admits that he was paid a £50,000 'promotion bonus' for getting the club to the Premiership, then took another £50,000 'payment' in the form of a year-long lease as a bonus for the club surviving in the Premiership so that he could run a top-of-the-range 6.5 litre Bentley Azure out of the club.

But he says, defiantly and forcibly, 'Yes, I did OK financially, but I risked my money at the beginning, back in 1994. I certainly don't apologise for taking dividends in proportion to my invested shareholding. That's something all

shareholders participate in. I am aware of the huge criticism over the dividend issue, but you have to remember I worked full time for six years and didn't draw a penny piece from the club until we were in the Premiership.

'Lots of club's chief executives would have expected four, five or six times the £250,000 fees I was paid for two years running when we were in the Premiership. I was offered £1 million to be chief executive of a Premiership club in 1999, but turned it down because of my vision of Bradford City's future.

'If I had said to supporters back in 1994, when we were in the third tier of football "Here's a £2.3 million loan, completely unsecured. If it all goes wrong, I lose it all and there's no claim against Bradford City. I'm going to work full time from 8am until 7pm for the next five or six years, and I'm not going to charge the club anything in payment or expenses. And if I'm right, and we get into the Premiership, would you have a problem with me drawing a dividend on shares that I've got and a salary for services thereafter? Is that unreasonable?" I think I know what the fans would have said.' Defiant as he is on the remuneration front, Richmond does admit that the building of the main Sunwin Stand, with a loan of £7.5 million to do so, 'was a major mistake'. Another cigarette hits his lips as he says 'It was too big a financial strain on the club, but it characterised my chairmanship. I wanted to improve both on and off the pitch, establish the club in the Premiership and give it the capacity to do so. However, the £7.5 million loan proved to be an albatross round our neck.'

As the club landed in administration in May 2002, both Richmond and the Rhodes family tried separately to buy the club. Initially, Yorkshire fun park owner Gordon Gibb offered to join Richmond, putting together a business plan, whereby Gibb put up the money and Richmond stayed as chairman. As events moved on, the rival would-be purchasers came together and with nine days to go to the 2002–03 season's kick-off, a verbal deal was discussed for a three-way split between Richmond, Gibb and the Rhodes family. The next day it all changed, as the 'Rhodes women' made their stand.

According to Richmond, Julian Rhodes told him that his mother and his sister objected strongly to him staying on at the club, and the pressure from them would be such that the Professor and Julian would have to pull out, although Julian Rhodes insists there was never any question of the Rhodes family doing that.

Richmond claims 'I had an awful dilemma. Did I stick to my guns, knowing the outcome, or walk away to allow a 50–50 deal to take place between Gordon Gibb and the Rhodes family? I didn't want to be the man who destroyed Bradford City, so I left the club with a heavy heart.'

According to Julian Rhodes, however, Richmond had no choice but to leave owing to a legal agreement that was signed prior to the club going into administration, and he found himself ousted by the Rhodes and Gibb families, who took control of the club.

Richmond was given guarantees that any liabilities in his name would be covered by the new partners, and so was free of any responsibilities. He was reported to have asked for £1 million for his shares, but denies this vehemently, stressing that he was paid a nominal £1 for them by Gibb. But he adds 'I went into my office on the following Monday and cleared my desk. As I drove away, I was in tears. It had been my life, and I have never been back since.'

So what are his thoughts today? He says 'I don't ever rule out coming back, but let history take its course. I think the club could make it to the top again – with a Geoffrey Richmond. But I'm in my mid-60s, and common sense tells me it will not happen. I would like nothing more, but the clock ticks and you grow older. I've had offers and lots of invitations, but everything would be second best to Bradford City. Nothing could match the emotional involvement. As the years go on, the administration period will fade away in people's thoughts, but the glory years will never do so. People will only remember the exciting period of the Premiership years.

'The Rhodes family have played a magnificent part in the history of the club. It's not a Richmonds versus the Rhodes situation. It's not about who was the good guy and who was the bad guy. I regret the ending, and I totally accept my shortcomings that led to administration, but I played my part too in lifting the whole city. It came alive and people were proud to be Bradford City supporters.'

SOLDIER BOY – Benito Carbone does pre-season training with the army.

THE RHODES TO RECOVERY

GEOFFREY RICHMOND may have been the public face and voice of Bradford City for so many years, but the Rhodes family was the ultimate financial backing.

Without Professor Rhodes – a leading academic and millionaire businessman – and his son, Julian, there would be no Bradford City today.

They provided the security and guarantees that helped to make the dream of Premiership football possible. They also provided much of the money to bail out the club when everything went pear-shaped.

The figures are beyond the ordinary fan's comprehension. Millions here, millions there, with much of it coming from the Rhodes family fortune.

True enough, they received substantial dividend payments in 1999 and 2000, along with the Richmond family, but the Rhodes family were still left massively out of pocket.

They had mainly used the wealth generated from the sale of shares in the family's successful Bradford-based, high-tech firm Filtronics, but finally Professor Rhodes and his wife had to put their family home forward as collateral. They even had to pay out more than half of their pension provision to see the club through to the end of the 2002–03 season.

During their eight years of involvement at Bradford City, Professor Rhodes and his son are credited with putting in £9 million in cash, with the Rhodes family also supplying about £20 million-worth of real security in the form of shares in their company, the family home of Professor and Mrs Rhodes and some hard cash. They have been paid back £3 million from the two dividends.

It all seems a far cry from those innocent and youthful days when young Julian became a ball boy at Valley Parade at the age of 11. He was introduced by Peter Jones, who ran the Otley Express football club, where Julian was a 'central-midfielder, turned lazy centre-forward'. Like any true fan, he still recalls watching his first senior game. He was eight years old, and City were playing Port Vale in the FA Cup. 'Terry Dolan scored a late winner from the penalty spot. I still remember it vividly,' says Julian.

His father first came along for that memorable victory against Liverpool in the League Cup in August 1980. Young Julian stood on a fishing stool in the old paddock, and when Bobby Campbell scored what proved to be the winner in the home leg Professor Rhodes was as hooked as his son.

They have been watching City ever since, and so hooked was Julian that in January 1997 he called Geoffrey Richmond with a view to investing some money in the club. Within half an hour a meeting was set up. The result was that Professor Rhodes and Julian bought 49 percent of the club's shares for a reputed £3 million. Today, Julian Rhodes candidly admits 'I didn't realise what we were letting ourselves in for.'

Some observers feel that the Rhodes family were far too naïve and far too hands-off in their initial approach, but the family preferred to keep a low profile, leaving Richmond to run the day-to-day footballing affairs in his hands-on manner. As Julian says, 'The original plan was for us to get involved to a greater extent than we did, but it soon became apparent that Geoffrey Richmond wanted to do things his way. Initially, we didn't have a problem with that. There was no outlandish investment and there were contingency plans if the club was relegated.'

Julian Rhodes also reveals 'During the summer of 1998 Geoffrey decided that the Division looked weak and that we should have a crack at promotion to the Premiership. He arranged for merchant bankers Singer and Friedlander to give us a £5 million facility to buy the players we required. Both Geoffrey and my father were guarantors, but we put up the £7.5 million Filtronic shares to give cover. We felt a bit

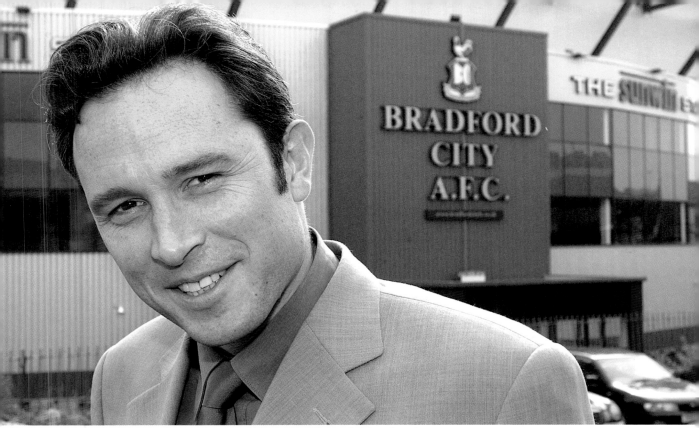

CITY SAVIOUR – Chairman Julian Rhodes, who guided City through two administration crises.

exposed, but the shares were doing well and it was not seen as a major risk.

'As everyone knows, we got promoted. We needed to expand the ground, and even before promotion we put up another £3 million-worth of Filtronic shares to pay for the new 7,300-seater Carlsberg Stand on the site of the Kop.

'In the first season in the Premier League, the wages bill and the transfer funding was done in such a way that had we been relegated we would have been strong enough financially in the lower Division.'

Also in that first season of the Premier League, the club decided to develop the ground still further and finance the second tier of the giant Sunwin Stand, with a rounded corner to link up with the two-tier Carlsberg Stand. In all, a mortgage of £7.5 million pounds was taken out with Lombards, with Geoffrey Richmond and Julian Rhodes standing as 'joint and several' guarantors.

The 'six weeks of madness' followed, and that's when the seeds of Bradford City's financial disaster were not only sewn but fertilised and watered. Players were brought in on long contracts and very high wages, and large amounts of money were borrowed through a scheme insured by the German insurance firm Gerling.

Julian Rhodes observes 'The problems came in that summer of 2000.' Benito Carbone was brought in on a reported £40,000 a week and on a four-year contract. The Rhodes family say they found out after the deal had been done in Italy; they, like the fans, were surprised at Richmond's audacity. The week before, Dan Petrescu had joined in a £1 million transfer from Chelsea, again on a four-year contract and high wages. Then there was Leeds United's David Hopkin, who cost £2.5 million, and Ashley Ward, who cost £1.5 million from Blackburn. Both were on very high wages, and Ward was on another four-year contract. In addition, Peter Atherton and Ian Nolan were signed on 'free transfers' from Sheffield Wednesday, although they were on Premiership wages.

Were the Rhodes family alarmed at the developments? Julian says 'All along we thought this guy knows what he's doing. We had no reason to think otherwise at that stage. In retrospect, we should have been more involved. To be fair, Geoffrey saw the club as being up there with names in lights, but with what he did that summer it was obvious that if relegation followed there would be massive problems.'

Relegation did follow and now the club faced

financial pressure on four fronts: quarterly mortgage repayments of £330,000 on the £7.5 million pound mortgage to Lombards for the incomplete main stand work; repayments to Benfield Greig (REFFS) of approximately £1.2 million a quarter; players wages of approximately £9 million on an annualised basis and the payments on the 26 separate leasing deals.

But before the fateful day of administration, the Rhodes family put up more security to try to stave off what now seemed inevitable. It was like a helter skelter ride of never-ending demands. According to Julian Rhodes, an overdraft was agreed for £5 million in March 2002 and this had to be secured by a further £7.5 million-worth of Filtronic shares.

Julian Rhodes now admits 'With the benefit of hindsight, perhaps we should have called in the administrators then, but you try to pull through in such circumstances. By early May it became obvious we couldn't get through. Everything seemed to be collapsing like a pack of cards: Carbone came back from Middlesbrough; there was no ITV Digital money to speak of. They compounded the problem, but they were not the total reason. The main reason was relegation.

'Now, here was my father – a professor, a CBE, an OBE, a Fellow of the Royal Society, facing this! He was very upset at what had happened, and ultimately even more upset when Geoffrey Richmond, according to Professor Rhodes, told him he was 'unable to help' in providing any finance whatsoever.

Again, the Rhodes family stumped up a further £400,000 to help make sure all the staff were paid until the end of June, before they battled to try to sort out the debts, the creditors and the money owed to players. Julian says 'It was an awful, awful period. The whole thing looked unviable.'

Eventually, the players were compensated for their loss of income through a deal with the Professional Footballers' Association using their hardship fund. This required payments to be made to the PFA by the club. The PFA wanted £1 million-worth of security, and the Rhodes family put forward the whole of this security, part of which was Professor Rhodes's family home. They also had to pay £3.2 million in cash to the bank, and then came the final pay-out of £430,000 from Professor Rhodes's' pension provision savings.

The eventual Rhodes-Gibb alliance was made after the summer, basically to take over the club on a 50–50 basis, with Julian Rhodes as the everyday hands-on working chief executive, and Gordon Gibb taking over the chairmanship. Richmond was not part of the final equation.

Still the problems went on. 'The projected gates and commercial activity figures for the following 2002–03 season proved to be wildly optimistic in the circumstances. We would be £2.25 million pounds down on expectation,' says Julian Rhodes. 'Fortunately, the players agreed to a 20 percent wage deferral; the PFA to a 50 percent deferral of moneys owing and a League grant of £330,000 was only forthcoming if we put in £430,000 – that's when my Mum and Dad's pension money was used.'

Even the stadium, shop and office building had to be sold and immediately leased back in order to pay a large proportion of the debt owed to Lombards. This was when the Gibb family pension fund was used to buy the stadium.

As everyone now knows, the Rhodes and Gibbs fell out big time, and the unravelling of the financial arrangements between the two parties was only completed after acrimonious exchanges and a second period of administration.

Rhodes admits 'As for my father and myself, we have changed over the last few years, hopefully for the wiser. It's fair to say we have been a bit naïve in the past, but we have learned from it and one good thing is that the summer of 2002 brought us closer together as we battled through the hard times.'

But still the dream remains, and he adds 'I just feel that we might get back in the big time one day, but with a realistic wage bill this time.'

MANAGER'S POINTS OF VIEW
FRANK STAPLETON

FRANK STAPLETON'S chance to become player-manager of Bradford City came right out of the blue – his sacking didn't.

The former Irish international reveals 'I liked dealing with Dave Simpson, the chairman who came in for me and appointed me, but when Geoffrey Richmond took over I knew on the first day that I wasn't going to last.'

Within four months the one-time Arsenal, Manchester United, Ajax and Blackburn Rovers player was turfed out of Valley Parade, 'as soon as we could no longer get in the play-offs'. Stapleton, who managed Bradford for two and a half years between December 1991 and May 1994, angrily refutes any suggestion that he didn't work hard enough at the job.

He may have had the more laid-back style of a seasoned pro, but says 'I did about 10 different jobs, including coaching the reserves. There was no reserve-team coach. I managed, coached, helped out our only scout and played as well. The resources at the club were poor, but I knew that was the case when I came. I have no resentment whatsoever against David Simpson. I got on very well with him.' In January 1994 Richmond took over and, according to Stapleton, 'He made no communication with me until the afternoon. He spent the first part of the day with the Press. I thought "This guy isn't interested in me. He hasn't shown me one iota of respect." I'd never met the guy before, but on the first day I knew it wasn't to be.

'At our first meeting he told me to sack the chief scout and the physio. I told him "No" on two accounts. Firstly, we needed them and, secondly, they had families to support. But Richmond told me to sack them, and that I had two weeks to do so. Two weeks later there was another row because I hadn't complied. Things got worse after that. They were circumstances you couldn't work under. The relationship was shocking, but there is only one winner in those circumstances and that's the chairman.' All these years on the feelings come flooding out of Stapleton, as though he's been waiting to get it off his chest. He goes on, 'When he sacked me he said he'd simply told the papers the bare facts and that was all, but he slaughtered me. I resented that and I resent any inference that I didn't work hard. That was ridiculous.'

Stapleton claims 'It was clear he wanted to be the manager. He wanted to run the team, the lot. He wanted puppets but knew I would never be that. Richmond set himself up as the great saviour of the club, and, to a certain extent, he succeeded, but at what cost? In my day there was nothing worse than an overdraft.'

contractual obligation with Waddle was that he could be released to be a first-team manager elsewhere, not as a player.

Another key event was the signing of Gordon Watson from Southampton in January for £550,000, but the player's career would be threatened three weeks later by an horrific injury following a tackle in a match at Valley Parade by Huddersfield Town defender Kevin Gray. Kamara says 'We had struggled to score goals that season. So, we went after Gordon. The Southampton manager Graeme Souness did me a massive favour by letting me have him on the cheap. I knew Gordon from his Sheffield Wednesday days, and I had played against him. I had also watched him play for Wednesday when I was a player at Sheffield United.

'To lose him after he had scored his first goal in the League match before was a bad blow. The club took out legal proceedings, and I had to give evidence in court. Gordon received a lot of money in compensation – £900,000. I didn't think he would come back from that. It was quite remarkable that he came back to play.'

Another key signing that season was goalkeeper Mark Schwarzer. Kamara says 'We signed Mark in the November from German club Kaiserslautern for £150,000, although the figure given out publicly was £325,000. Mark did well for us, but we sold him to Middlesbrough for £1.335 million the following February. So, he was with us for only four months, but there was a clause in his contract to say that if received an offer of more than £1 million we had to put it to him.

'I thought he was going to be the best goalkeeper in Europe, and I told him that. He has had great success, but I thought he would be at Arsenal or Manchester United by now.'

Meanwhile, Kamara's side were battling against relegation and found themselves having to win their last two matches – at home to Charlton and QPR – to ensure their survival. The Bantams had lost 2–0 at Barnsley on the penultimate Saturday

of the season – a result that took Barnsley into the Premiership. Then, City beat Charlton 1–0 in their game in hand on General Election day of 1997, and beat QPR 3–0 on the final day of the season, with midfield player Nigel Pepper, a £103,000 signing from York, scoring three goals. City needed that victory over QPR because their relegation rivals Grimsby also won, but were relegated two points behind City.

Kamara says 'I never felt we would go down, and it took me by surprise that we had to beat Charlton on the Thursday before the last match of the season against QPR on the Sunday to stay in the First Division. The object of the exercise was to finish fourth from the bottom and then plan for the following season.

'The result of staying up was almost as big an achievement as going up the year before. Geoffrey Richmond wanted to stabilise and that's what we did.'

City had signed striker Robbie Blake from Darlington on transfer deadline day for £300,000, and during the summer Kamara strengthened the squad further by signing Peter Beagrie for a knock-down £50,000 from Manchester City, Jamie Lawrence for £50,000 from Leicester City and Darren Moore for a tribunal-fixed £310,000 from Doncaster Rovers.

They were all considered to be successful signings. One signing that was not successful was Bolton striker John McGinlay, bought for £625,000. Kamara says 'The following season we were short of goals and needed to sign a goalscorer. I thought McGinlay was the man. I had seen him scoring goals for Bolton, but he didn't do himself justice at Bradford City. We checked him out medically and he seemed fine, but, in my final game – a third-round FA Cup tie at Manchester City – he missed three wonderful chances.'

Those misses effectively cost Kamara his job. It was inconceivable that he would have been sacked with City still in the Cup, but sacked he was two days later and another managerial era at Valley Parade came to an end.

PAUL JEWELL

MANAGER Paul Jewell couldn't believe his ears. His newly-promoted Bradford City side had survived in the Premiership and here was his chairman Geoffrey Richmond telling him at their so-called celebratory lunch 'You've had a bad season. Your tactical naivety has cost us points.'

Just a couple of months earlier, after a 4–0 defeat at Coventry, Jewell claims Richmond told him 'If you're contract was up, you wouldn't get it renewed.'

Relations had become strained between the former Liverpool apprentice and Bradford City striker and the ambitious, up-front, hands-on chairman, who revelled in high-profile publicity, notoriety and the sheer exhilaration and status of being a Premiership chairman with a seat at the top table. Now, as they sat together in the fashionable Clark's restaurant on the west side of Bradford, their end-of-season lunch together was anything but celebratory.

After steering his 'relegation certainties' to their last day victory over his old club Liverpool to ensure Bradford City another season in the coveted top flight, Jewell was expecting a pat on the back or at least a convivial meeting. It was anything but, though by now Jewell was getting used to the ways of chairman Richmond.

Jewell recalls 'In the restaurant, I showed him my list of players I would like to bring in. He looked at it and told me he'd never disagreed with a manager so much over players I wished to move on.

'After this, he told me he wanted to take Bradford into Europe via the Inter-Toto Cup. When he told me the competition kicked-off in July, I told him it was a crazy idea. The players had given their all and needed as long a break as possible, but he was adamant.

'Then he told me I'd had a bad season and had cost the club vital points because of my tactical naivety, an in-phrase at the time. I stood up to him and asked him 'Was it tactical naivety that brought us victory over Arsenal, Newcastle and Liverpool? In my opinion, it was a disgraceful charge and it upset me greatly.'

That was the very moment that Paul Jewell, the manager who had made history by leading Bradford into the promised land, decided to quit the club that meant so much to him. He reveals 'I decided I was leaving there and then. It was not doing my health any good.'

On the soccer grapevine, it was known that First Division Sheffield Wednesday were after a manager of Jewell's standing, but was it conceivable that a Premiership manager would willingly take a drop down in Division, status and money?

Jewell, seeing that the way ahead at Bradford would only be more angst-ridden for him, came out of Clark's and immediately rang a friend to ask him if there was still a vacancy at Sheffield Wednesday.

In the end, Jewell went away on holiday for two weeks, came back and told Richmond to his face that he was quitting the club. He says 'I didn't like what I had become. In my opinion, I was chosen from within the club so that Richmond could try to keep overall control. The more experienced and the stronger I became, the more the relationship frayed at the edges. I appealed to him to trust me more but he wanted control.

'I'm not ungrateful. He gave me my first job, but I repaid him well. He gave me my first chance, but I don't owe him anything now. I took the side into the Premiership and made the club a lot of money. If he has any criticism of me, I want to put the record straight.'

When Jewel was asked to take up the reins at debt-ridden Sheffield Wednesday, a club in crisis on and off the field, it was put about that he had quit Bradford for greed, with rumours that he had doubled his salary. But Jewell insists 'I can honestly say that I earned less money at Sheffield Wednesday than I did at Bradford.'

Jewell also readily admits that it was certainly not a career move. 'I went for the wrong reasons, to get away from the difficulties of my job at Bradford. It was not a happy situation at Wednesday, and I knew I was in a no-win situation, but I was away.'

Jewell reveals that a previous Bradford City manager had warned him that Richmond 'sucked the energy from you', but even then he was unprepared for what he describes as 'the relentless meetings' almost every single day.

At one Monday morning inquest, after the heavy defeat at Coventry, Jewell says that the chairman had yet another list in front of him. Jewell reveals 'He accused me of getting my tactics wrong, of not scouting well enough and of being on TV too much, which was rich coming from him. He'd walk a million miles to be on telly! He accused me of making a fool of him in front of an agent, simply because I wasn't convinced that we needed the German goalkeeper he was peddling. I told him that he took more notice of agents than me anyway.

'Then he turned the page of his list and the rest of what happened astounded me. Our next match was at home against Manchester United and Geoffrey had it all worked out. We would play 4-3-3, go a goal up and then change the formation and hold them until half-time. Then we would go on and, if memory serves me well, we would beat them 4-0. If it wasn't serious it would be funny.

'Needless to say, our relationship was deteriorating. I didn't feel I was managing the club. I was becoming a puppet, and when I stood up for myself there were rows and what I considered to be intimidation. Remember, he also told me that if my contract had been up I wouldn't get it renewed. He was draining me. I would come home tired and dispirited.'

Jewell knew it would be tough in the Premiership and adds 'I always said it was a big 'ask', and I feel our achievements are still not given enough credit. We had been Christened 'Dad's Army' because we had a team of older, experienced players, but it worked. The critics said we couldn't hack it but we stayed up to fight on.

'We had signed David Wetherall for £1.4million from Leeds; Gunnar Halle for £200,000; Lee Sharpe from Leeds for £200,000; Dean Saunders, a free from Benfica and Matt Clarke, on a Bosman free from Sheffield Wednesday and, of course, we had Stuart McCall, with some sceptics questioning his ability to achieve at this level!

'It was a marvellous feeling to shock everyone by winning our first Premiership game, away at Middlesbrough, through a Dean Saunders goal. Then we faced Sheffield Wednesday at home and got a point – a good start. Soon afterwards, the chairman took me out to Clark's for a meal and said 'One day, you'll be the England manager. I burst out laughing, but when I looked at him he was serious. He was often unrealistic about soccer life. Still, the champagne tasted good.'

Jewell added 'It was always going to be a problem scoring goals. At Premiership level it's so much more difficult. The chairman thought we should always attack teams. We did at Arsenal and were two down in 15 minutes. It could have been 20-0 by the end. I knew we had to be tight. We didn't want demoralising, big-score defeats. Morale would really be shot at then. But all the time I was having to undergo discussions and meetings virtually every afternoon with Richmond. They would start at 1pm and often go on until 6pm.

'In addition, Geoffrey loved agents and rubbing shoulders with the big names in football. Take the case of Isaiah Rankin, an Arsenal reserve who I rated was worth a punt for about £50,000 when we were in the First Division in my first full season in charge. In the end, Geoffrey paid £1.3 million. But top of the chairman's list at the time was Samassi Abou at West Ham. Yet Abou didn't speak good English, they wanted £800,000 for him, and I hadn't seen him play, to which Geoffrey replied "You've watched *Match of the Day* haven't you?" He then asked me if I would come down to London with him to sign him? Now I thought that managers chose players, but this was the start.'

WE'VE DONE IT – Geoffrey Richmond celebrates with Stuart McCall and Paul Jewell outside City Hall before a civic reception to celebrate promotion to the Premiership.

The daily quiz on tactics or selection began in earnest, leading to the point a year on where Jewell was accused of showing 'tactical naivety'. The former Liverpool apprentice, who had learned his trade alongside the likes of Kenny Dalglish and Ian Rush, and under the tutelage of Bob Paisley, Joe Fagan and the famous Anfield 'boot room' brigade, admits mistakes were made and that he should have stood his ground more and stuck out against the pressure. But when questioning him on his footballing brain, he retorts 'I've forgotten more about the game than Richmond will ever know.'

Interestingly, on the Isaiah Rankin front, Jewell claims that his original idea to go for him, offering £50,000, was pooh-poohed by Richmond, but was reactivated after Richmond's son David met England coach Peter Taylor on holiday and asked him for his opinion. Jewell claims 'Geoffrey loved talking to David Dein and Arsene Wenger and paid £1.3 million for Rankin. At a push, I would have paid £200,000.'

Yet Jewell went along with it all, and he should have known what was coming his way in management. He had been at the club as a player well before Richmond took over and had learned

the hard way how things can change. Jewell had reported back for training in 1995, only to find his No.6 training kit had been given to Eddie Youds. Jewell was given old kit with holes in it and told to train on his own. 'Maybe it was the club trying to get me out,' says Jewell. 'It was not a professional way to deal with the issue. To be treated like that is appalling.'

He knuckled down anyway, and, after loan periods away, was rehabilitated when Chris Kamara took over from Lennie Lawrence as manager. Jewell says 'Ultimately, I went on the coaching staff. I often did the half-time talks too. Then, one day, Chris told me the chairman had asked his secretary to get the staff contracts out after we had had a bit of a wobble, being knocked out of the FA Cup by Manchester City. Kamara went up to see Richmond and returned in a state of shock. He had been sacked, and Richmond wanted to see me!

'He asked me to look after the team, and when we won my first game in charge he rang me and said "I'll be rushing round slowly looking for a new manager." Then, mid-conversation, he shouted out "You b-----d!" He had just heard David Mellor on BBC Radio 5 Live asking

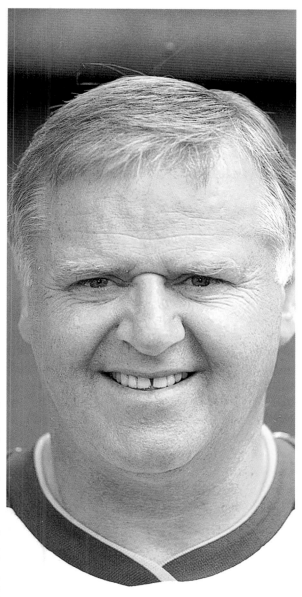

confidence in my ability and my track record. We don't have any money at Kilmarnock, but we get on with the job and we don't get any interference. I really enjoy it. It is a good little club to work for. The only blip on my CV was at Bradford City, but it was an experience I didn't regret.'

'One of the players Jeffries inherited at Valley Parade was Italian Benito Carbone. Jeffries says 'I was very honest with Carbone from the start. He wanted to get back to Italy and the chairman knew that. He was a big burden on the club's wage bill, but he was a terrific lad. We lived pretty near each other at Leeds, and I went to his house a couple of times, but he wasn't the type of player Bradford should have been signing. He was talented, but we didn't have the players to accommodate him.

'In my opinion, the club was the chairman's toy – his life. He had had a lot of success and he was well thought of because of that, but it seemed that everything was short term and it became a situation that was pretty hopeless. I realised very early I never had the chance to do the job my way. I was sorry to hear about the slide into administration, but you can't blame the players for accepting the big contracts – I would have taken them as well. I am not saying the players were not worth it, but they put the club in a difficult financial position. You just have to write it off to experience.'

Jeffries is certainly critical of City's training facilities while he was there. He says 'You bring quality players into the club and then take them to the sort of training facilities we had and you demotivate them straightaway. I tried to improve these things, and I took the players to a new training ground that was not fantastic but was better. You have no chance to make the team better with poor training facilities. There was also no youth policy and, in my opinion, no adequate scouting system.

'It seemed to me there was no long-term thinking in the way I would have wished. I wanted to do well for the club, but the things I was told before I took the job turned out to be correct. I learned the hard way.'

but I felt it was unwise to go down that path. We cleared a lot of money off the wage bill, but I never got the chance to build it further. I wasn't surprised that Robbie Blake was sold to Burnley just after I left. I didn't want to sell him unless I got the money to replace him.

'I had been successful at other clubs before getting the Bradford job, and I have been successful in difficult circumstances at Kilmarnock, but the people I work with have

NICKY LAW

NICKY LAW was never one to pull back from a tackle when he was a player, but when he became manager of Bradford City on 31 December 2001 he had to tackle a New Year challenge of a lifetime.

It's a long time ago since the one-time Arsenal apprentice stepped through the marbled halls of Highbury, but since those heady days he had become used to the rough and tumble of soccer life at places like Barnsley, Rotherham, Notts County and Chesterfield.

Even so, in your second job as a manager you don't expect to be handling crisis after crisis on an almost daily basis. His management skills were put on public trial as he took control of a club in critical condition.

With a wage bill draining the club to alarming levels and the side sliding towards what would have been a second successive relegation, the task was hard enough. He had to handle inherited players like Benito Carbone, who, through no fault of his own, was paid an enormous amount and was still only half way through his four-year contract. When he refused transfer chances to Premier League clubs, Law had to handle the situation, knowing it was potentially disruptive, not to mention costly.

With safety in Division One achieved, Law then faced an even bigger crisis as the club were in danger of going bust during the close season of 2002, with players not being paid and creditors putting pressure on the stricken club. In the midst of all this, Law had to shelve any plans for bringing in new players, while protecting and motivating his existing staff. Somehow, he managed to encourage them sufficiently to train pre-season, not knowing who would remain at the club, or if there would be a club at all when the new season kicked-off.

Yet Law remained as philosophical as ever, having kept the Bantams in Division One, which was probably the equivalent of gaining promotion in the circumstances. He admitted 'It was a difficult time for the club and there is no doubt we had a long and tough season as we came out of administration. There was not much money to spend, but I realised the situation when I came and it was a real challenge. Considering the circumstances, achieving survival with a few games left to spare was not a bad achievement.'

Law became reconciled to losing most of his players who were out of contract, although he kept senior players like David Wetherall and Wayne Jacobs to steer the club through the 2003–04 season. An average wage cap of £1,500 a week had been imposed, so Law was having to work within a realistic framework. The emphasis at the club was on youth, and home-grown youth wherever possible.

Law blooded several young stars over the final two months of that season, a move that was necessary but still bold and often inspired. The likes of local lad Danny Forrest, who used to support City on the Kop; Simon Francis, picked up by youth scouts in Nottingham, and Ben Muirhead, who has moved to Valley Parade from Manchester United, all had their chance to prove their worth in the first team.

Law is used to picking himself up and getting on with his life. It must have hurt to leave Arsenal, the club where he turned professional in 1979, after failing to make it to the first team. He went on to make his mark in soccer at Barnsley, Blackpool, Plymouth, Notts County, Scarborough, Rotherham, Chesterfield, where he would ultimately became manager, and finally Hereford United.

After great success at Saltergate, he was brought in by Geoffrey Richmond to lift the gloom at Bradford. He said at the time 'I'm still convinced we can get this club going again. It's only a short time ago since they were in the Premiership and the aim has got to be returning there at some point.'

knew this level of payment was academic and pointed out that the longer Gibb delayed, the longer the delay in him getting his annual £300,000 rent for the ground.

Rhodes knew that the final vote against would come from ex-player Ashley Ward, who was claiming £832,000. And crucially, with Ward's vote against, there was no chance of getting agreement to a CVA deal. As Rhodes says 'Suddenly, we didn't have a 75 percent majority.'

Could one of the 'No' voters be turned? As the noon deadline approached, Rhodes met the Inland Revenue representative, to no avail. What about Ashley Ward? He couldn't be contacted in time, so Rhodes bought time by getting the noon meeting adjourned for an hour, then for three hours. It wasn't long enough to get everyone on board, though ultimately Rhodes made a deal with Ward, who accepted 20p in the pound of what he was owed, which still amounted to around £135,000.

In a bid to smooth the Inland Revenue, Rhodes went to see them the following week, and even though they faced being paid only 1p in the pound, the meeting seemed to work because they didn't appeal against the CVA terms.

The Gibb aspect proved more difficult. Understandably, he was reluctant to see his family pension fund investment turn to dust. He was obliged to try to protect it anyway and wanted personal guarantees from Rhodes, which he was not prepared to give.

Gibb appealed against the CVA, though Rhodes clearly didn't think he had any chance of success. His solicitors went to court, but the case was adjourned. Both parties played a waiting game, and though there was some nastiness from some fans, who saw Gibb as a stumbling block rather than see his side of the story, Rhodes stayed relaxed and tried to remain focused on football. Oh yes. The drama might be off the pitch, but at least football was being played at Valley Parade.

In November, Gibb's people dropped the issue about personal guarantees, and an agreement was drafted to suit both parties. The CVA was re-convened on 9 December 2004 with Lombard's, Ward, the FA and the Football League on board and everything signed up. Naturally, there was a last-minute hitch, but eventually the deal was signed at lunchtime the following day, and a new company set up – Bradford City Football Club Ltd.

Out of administration, two issues remained – players' wage deferments, amounting to £350,000, and the issue of the £1 million owed to the lease creditors who owned most of the equipment and fittings at the ground. Both matters were addressed, the players accepting either new contractual deals or extended deferment terms. Some lease creditors accepted deals, others did not.

But as Rhodes says, 'At last we can concentrate on trading as a solvent football club, aiming to progress back up the Football League. And despite all the events off the field, last season saw a remarkable achievement on the field of play. I thought we might be looking at another relegation while our financial affairs and the CVA were being sorted out, and that I would have to pull the club back from League Two. Yet, against the odds, we were disappointed to miss out on the play-offs, even though the bookies predicted we would be second bottom.'

It had taken two and a half years to solve the club's financial problems, and at the same time the Rhodes family also saw the family fortune diminish, with shares in their high-tech firm Filtronic losing 99 percent of their value at one point. Rhodes admits 'Over that period I went through periods of despair and insomnia trying to figure out how I could keep the club going, but I look back on it with a great feeling of satisfaction and excitement at what I think we can achieve in the future. I feel battle hardened. I feel like saying Come on, bring it on. Throw it at me. We can deal with anything here!'

SUPPORTERS TO THE RESCUE...

IN THE LIMELIGHT – Bulls coach Brian Noble (front row, left) joins fans taking part in the pro-celebrity fund raising day at Valley Parade.

THE FANS played a crucial role in keeping the club going through the agonising period of the second administration. They raised over £250,000 in all, the single biggest fundraising effort ever by fans of a UK football club. It not only played a major part in the club's survival, but it also proved that the Bradford public cared about the club. That was perhaps more important than the amount raised. Here, local journalist Andrew Hebden reveals how it happened...

IT had all begun with a relative whimper. As the club's predicament became all the more uncertain, a number of the rapidly-dwindling group of staff remaining in the Valley Parade offices decided they couldn't simply stand by and watch as their club folded before them.

Hastily, they decided to stage a stunt to raise the profile of their plight and frantically rang round the local media to tell them of a planned roof-top protest at the ground.

Newspaper and radio journalists joined film crews at the scene, only to find that the staff had pulled out due to 'health and safety considerations.' It was not exactly the resolve of Sherpa Tensing! Instead, the staff waved banners and flags at passing cars. It stirred a few disgruntled motorists but failed to hit the headlines.

However, the move did have a major effect, which would have profound repercussions on the battle for City's survival. It encouraged the Bradford City Supporters' Trust to seize the momentum and organise their own protest. They called for a 'silent vigil' and urged fans to gather at the ground, where they would blow whistles to attract attention to City's financial problems.

Volunteers spent the night of Wednesday 12 May fastening makeshift posters and banners – thrown together from old sheets and pieces of discarded cardboard – to just about every bridge